Your eco-friendly Yard

SUSTAINABLE IDEAS TO SAVE YOU TIME, MONEY AND THE EARTH

Tom Girolamo

Copyright ©2009 Tom Girolamo

Published by

krause publications

A subsidiary of F+W Media, Inc.

700 East State Street • Iola, WI 54990-0001
715-445-2214 • 888-457-2873
www.krausebooks.com

Our toll-free number to place an order or obtain
a free catalog is (800) 258-0929.

Neither the author nor Krause Publications assumes any liability for uses made of the metric information presented. All units are approximate.

Cover photography by Kris Kandler

Library of Congress Control Number: 2008941159

ISBN 13: 978-1-4402-0242-1
ISBN 10: 1-4402-0242-7

Cover design by: Heidi Zastrow
Interior design by: Rachael Knier
Edited by: Candy Wiza

Printed in China

Mission statement: Enjoy the simple things in life while you reduce, reuse and recycle.

Printed on 100% recycled paper

DEDICATION

To my wife, Kathy, who is a constant supporter of what I choose to do.
Your thoughtful advice and suggestions have kept me
out of trouble and off the streets all these years.

ACKNOWLEDGMENTS

I want to thank the following people and businesses for their commitment to me as a true believer in sustainable living and for their generous support:

- Candy Wiza, editor, Kris Kandler, photographer, and all of the staff at Krause Publications, for their trust in me and for taking the time and effort to help me, a new author, through the book writing process.
- Terry Misfeldt from Simply Success in Green Bay, Wis., for helping me recognize the importance of lifestyle and personality in creating sustainable landscapes, creating the Lifestyle Pyramid and offering suggestions for some of my writing.
- Rainy Day Worzella from ArtVillage in Stevens Point, Wis., for the finishing work on the Lifestyle Pyramid.
- Jeanne McManus from Unirac, Inc., for supplying sketches for some of the solar equipment that is shown in the book.
- John Hippensteel from Lake Michigan Wind and Sun, for providing the sketch for the solar lighting shown in this book and photos of Solar Flairs™.
- My past employees, family, friends and supportive customers, for helping me learn more about the evolving sustainable landscape. It wouldn't be the same if you hadn't participated.
- University of Wisconsin - Stevens Point, Trainer College of Natural Resources, for the education in natural resources that set me on this path. My continued involvement and contact with UWSP has helped me benefit from the work and ongoing research by the University and its students for sustainability.
- I've been re-energized by Permaculture experts, Geoff Lawton and Nadia Abu Yahia of Permaculture Research Institute, Australia and Darren J. Doharty of Australia Felix Permaculture. Classes and visits by these Australians were sponsored by Global Environmental Management (GEM) located in Stevens Point, Wis.
- Jeffrey A. Thornton of International Environmental Management Services Limited, for his international perspective and his input and support of my alternative view of natural resource management.
- LeAnn S. Colburn of Environmental Horizons, Inc., for her expertise regarding water and soil issues provided in this book.

TABLE OF CONTENTS

[11]   **INTRODUCTION**

[13]   **CHAPTER 1: AN ECO-FRIENDLY YARD TO THE RESCUE**
     [13]   There's No Time to Lose
     [15]   A Different Approach
     [15]   It's All About You

[17]   **CHAPTER 2: TOP 10 THINGS TO AVOID IN AN ECO-FRIENDLY YARD**
     [17]   One Rain Barrel or Rain Garden
     [18]   Retaining Walls
     [19]   Compost Piles or Bins
     [19]   Removal of Organic Materials
     [20]   Rototilling
     [20]   Gardening
     [21]   Organic Fertilizers
     [21]   Advice From the Local Garden Shop
     [23]   What Someone Else Wants for You
     [23]   Native Plants

[25]   **CHAPTER 3: B.E.L.S.**
     [25]   Benefits
     [26]   Efficiency
     [29]   Lifestyle
     [30]   Systems

[33]   **CHAPTER 4: INTEGRATING HOME AND LANDSCAPE**
     [33]   Integrating Energy
     [37]   Integrating Structures

[41]   **CHAPTER 5: PLANNING AND DESIGN**
     [41]   The Property Owner Questionnaire
     [42]   Key to the Questionnaire
         [42]   Property Information
         [43]   Decision Makers
         [43]   Budgeting
         [45]   Design Analysis
     [47]   Choosing a Plan That's Right for You
     [47]   Design — The Continual Process

[49] CHAPTER 6: TOOLS THAT WORK SO YOU DON'T HAVE TO (*or at least not as hard*)
- [49] **Junk**
- [49] **Using the Right Tools**
- [50] **Better and Faster**
- [51] **High Tech Really Matters**
- [53] **Less is More**

[55] CHAPTER 7: PERSONALITY APPROACH TO A LIFESTYLE LANDSCAPE
- [55] **What's Your Lifestyle?**
- [59] **Using the Sustainable Lifestyle Pyramid**
- [61] **The Basic Four**

[63] CHAPTER 8: THE BOLD PERSONALITY
- [65] **Projects For Bold Personalities**
  - [65] Solar Electric Fence
  - [69] Solar Panel for Lighting and Pumps
  - [73] Large Solar Panel
  - [79] Micro-Irrigation
  - [85] Advanced Entertainment Areas
  - [87] Brick Oven
  - [91] Thin-Crust Pizza in the Brick Oven
  - [95] Benefits of Projects for Bold Personalities
  - [96] Plants for the Bold Personality

[99] CHAPTER 9: THE FUN PERSONALITY
- [101] **Projects for Fun Personalities**
  - [101] Outdoor Shower
  - [107] Wire Spool Bistro Table
  - [113] Bistro Chairs
  - [117] Cork End Table
  - [123] Benefits of Projects for Fun Personalities
  - [124] Plants for the Fun Personality

[127] CHAPTER 10: THE PERFECTIONIST PERSONALITY
- [129] **Projects for Perfectionist Personalities**
  - [129] Drip Irrigation
  - [133] Drip Irrigation for Planters
    - **[134] Determining Ample Water Supply for Drip Irrigation System**
    - **[135] How Long and How Often Should I Run My Irrigation System**
  - [136] Maintenance for Drip and Micro-Irrigation Systems
  - [138] "Blowing Out" Irrigation Lines
  - [141] Well-Organized Tool Storage
  - [143] Master Tool Storage
  - [147] Benefits of Projects for Perfectionist Personalities
  - [148] Plants for the Perfectionist Personality

[151] CHAPTER 11: THE EASY-GOING PERSONALITY

    [152] Projects for Easy-Going Personalities

        [152] Types of Mulch

        [153] Composting or Decomposition

        [155] Weed Control Prior to Mulching

        [156] The Black Plastic Myth for Reducing Weeds

        [156] Avoid Synthetic Weed Barriers

        [157] Easy Mulching and Composting

        [159] Fast and Easy Mulched Path

        [163] Sticks and Branches Mulch

        [167] Easy Weed Smothering

        [170] Plants That Make Mulch

        [171] Adding Plants to Self-Mulch Areas

        [173] Grow Ground Cover Plants

        [175] Chop-and-Drop Mulching Method

        [178] Benefits of Projects for Easy-Going Personalities

        [180] Plants for the Easy-Going Personality

[183] CHAPTER 12: PUT WATER TO WORK FOR YOU

    [185] Our Water Dilemma

        [187] Reducing Lawn Areas to Reduce Water Use

        [188] Water Use in the Home

        [189] Water and Your Lifestyle

        [190] Water with Benefits

    [192] Catch the Wave

        [192] Roof Materials

        [193] Gutters, Valleys and Eaves

        [193] Driveways, Patios and Other Impervious Surfaces

    [195] Swales

    [197] Ponds

        [197] Ponds Without Synthetic Liners

        [201] Ponds With Synthetic Liners

    [204] Water Tanks

    [204] Putting It All Together

[207] CHAPTER 13: TOP 10 MUST-HAVE ITEMS FOR CREATING YOUR ECO-FRIENDLY YARD

    [207] The Masonry Heater

    [209] Large Water Storage

    [210] Grow Perennial Food Crops

    [210] Share Your Sustainable Lifestyle

    [211] Grow Weeds

    [212] Raise Pet Chickens

    [213] Create Nature

    [214] Give Naysayers the Cold Shoulder

    [215] Make It Fit Your Personality and Your Lifestyle

    [217] Accept Change in Your Landscape

[219] CHAPTER 14: WHERE IN THE WORLD ARE YOU?
   [220] Learn From Your Environment - Past and Present
      [220] The Simple Life from Years Past
      [221] The Advent of Central Heat and Air Conditioning
      [221] Home, Business and Animal Shelters Constructed for Climate
      [222] Your Ancestors' Diet
      [222] Decay-Resistant Trees
      [224] Changes in Your Soil
      [225] Reuse, Reduce, Recycle
   [227] Health Benefits from Your Yard
      [227] Play in Your Yard
      [232] How Does Your Garden Grow?

[235] CHAPTER 15: SAFETY
   [235] Your Unique Situation
      [235] You Will Be Doing Things
      [235] Your Climate and Geographic Area
      [236] Your Culture or the Cultures of Those Around You
      [237] Sensitive Environments
   [239] Tool and Equipment Safety
   [241] Call Before You Dig
   [242] Plant Safety
   [243] Laws, Regulations and Permits
   [245] Surveys

[246] ZONE MAP

[247] METRIC TABLE

[248] GLOSSARY

[251] RESOURCES AND SUPPLIES

[252] INDEX

[255] ABOUT THE AUTHOR

Introduction
More Green for You

As I write the introduction to this special book, the financial markets have just collapsed, stocks are in the tank, and people who thought they had retirements, don't. It almost seems that we expect this sort of thing to happen. When we purchase a car, we expect it to depreciate by 50 percent a year. Our computers are outdated and worthless almost as soon as we take them out of the box. Lots of people are paying more for cell phone service and text messaging than they pay to heat and cool their home. Some new studies show that even good paying jobs end up earning close to minimum wage once the cost of work clothes, commuting and eating out is considered. Why are we working so hard when the biggest resource we have sits idle not earning a cent?

How many people do you know that make an investment, spend thousands a year maintaining it, actually work at reducing its value, never enjoy a penny of return and are fine with this happening? That investment is the biggest one you will ever make. Is this you?

The biggest investment you'll ever make is not your home; it is the property that surrounds your home. The average suburban lot uses more pesticides, more water, more fossil fuel and more time for maintenance per acre than even the most intensely managed agricultural land. If you have a standard lawn and landscape, the amount of energy and time that goes into maintaining this landscape will exceed the amount of energy and time required to build your home as well as exceeding the ongoing maintenance costs of the home. How can this be? Because the value of the area outside the home has been ignored and misunderstood. Low-cost energy has allowed our society to make decisions about their property based on whims of the moment. Well, that's not the way it will work anymore — there's no time to lose in making the change to an eco-friendly yard.

You can start right now with a sustainable landscape investment that you can see, use, smell, control and play in every day. You will feel safe in it, have the security of actually owning it, and know that you will make the best decisions for how it will be used. The best part is, no one can take this away from you.

Take your biggest asset, your property, and turn it into a powerhouse of benefits that you can use everyday. As long as you do it right, you will never use up this investment and it will flourish and multiply the whole time you are using it. But how do you do this?

This book is going to help you find those answers and help you create that eco-friendly yard and lifestyle that you have always wanted!

Chapter 1
An Eco-Friendly Yard to The Rescue

THERE'S NO TIME TO LOSE

My wife, Kathy, and I live, work and play in a northern climate where it can get down to -30° F (-34°C) during the winter and over 100° F (38°C) during the summer. We can have deluges of rain or drought for months and our growing season might only be 90 days between killing frosts. Yet, our landscape, home and lives are integrated in a way that we are surrounded by lush plants, produce a huge variety of foods on our own property, have a great time entertaining and cooking outside and we even make money from what we grow in our landscape. If we can do these things in one of the most varied climates in the world, imagine what you can accomplish in your own eco-friendly yard.

As we continue to commit resources to sustainable practices on our property, the cost of heating and cooling our home continues to drop, we spend less time maintaining what we have, we have more free time to pursue our passions and we are having more fun than ever before.

Does any of this sound interesting to you? Who wouldn't want more time, money or to have more fun? Take advantage of what your property has to offer. The place where you live may be different than mine and you may have even more resources than I do just waiting to be tapped.

It is easy to see why many landscapes are not meeting expectations. Every day people tell me they are dissatisfied and frustrated with their current landscape. How does a standard landscape benefit you? Does mowing a big yard make you happy? For some people it does. Where else can a guy drive in circles for hours, not ask directions and not get nagged about it? Others don't find it meaningful to do a task like mowing and would rather spend their time doing something else.

Some people are concerned that there is a lot of meaningless rhetoric about sustainability and how it can really benefit them, and I agree. There is a lot of "greenwash" (sort of like hogwash) out there with all sorts of claims being made by business, government and non-profits alike. What isn't claimed to be green, organic or sustainable now? All sorts of companies, products and services have jumped on the bandwagon. There are people telling others what they should do and this has led to confusion. Especially when those who are doing the telling aren't doing!

The way things are going right now, there is no time to lose in creating the eco-friendly yard that will produce benefits beyond your dreams. Starting now means you start benefiting now. Every day that goes by is another opportunity to create what will benefit you.

The word "organic," as defined by the USDA, is 52 pages long and lists all of the pesticides, chemicals and drugs, and all of the non-organic ingredients, that can be used in organic products.

A DIFFERENT APPROACH

What gets people excited is that I take a different approach to sustainability. If we remove all of the clutter from the definitions, **sustainable can simply be defined as something that truly benefits you.** Of course, a true benefit wouldn't hurt you, others or the environment. So, fast food with its fat and empty calories is not a true benefit no matter how convenient. Neither are all of the prescription drugs with the nasty side effects that are regularly dispensed when some simple lifestyle changes would have worked better. A true benefit would be one that has only positive effects to your mind, body and soul and fits your desired lifestyle. If it's a true benefit, it will help others and be good to the environment too.

IT'S ALL ABOUT YOU

Whether you call it a garden, yard, property, sustainable, green or organic it's about meeting your needs, how you want to live and the way you want to do it. You have my permission to read and use this book any way you want. Read it back to front, jump around, pick out the things you like best and do them right away or just glean the details that will make your yard more eco-friendly than it already is.

Chapter 2

Top 10 Things to Avoid in an Eco-Friendly Yard

You can make good progress on your eco-friendly yard, but not if you get bogged down in the clutter that we hear daily about what others think we should do in the name of sustainability. Many things that you might hear are just "green" sound-bites that aren't any different than phrases uttered by politicians. Let's cut through the clutter!

Many of the things on my Top 10 List are methods or systems that gardeners have been brainwashed into believing. Why waste your time and money doing things that may not provide true benefits for your eco-friendly yard? This list may upset some people and that's okay. It will only be the ones who were trying to control you by having you do meaningless things.

ONE RAIN BARREL OR RAIN GARDEN

What benefit will you get from either of these examples? In our Midwest climate, the average roof on a home and attached garage at 2,000 square feet (186m²) will generate at least 32,000 gallons (1,211hl) of run-off from precipitation per year. Is anybody really going to empty their 50-gallon (189L) rain barrel 640 times in order to capture and reuse all of that free water? If you spent only five minutes emptying the rain barrel, in this example, you would use up over 53 hours of your time per year. Is that time well spent? Most rain gardens I see just end up as weedy holes in the yard. Sometimes, they are soaking wet and other times bone dry and many plants do not tolerate these conditions. I do believe in starting small to experiment. If a rain barrel fits your lifestyle for a particular application, by all means try it. Just remember, the idea is to take advantage of free water in an efficient way.

This low-grow fragrant sumac will eventually cover this retaining wall. The same plant can be used to hold soil on a slope in place.

RETAINING WALLS

Retaining walls in most landscapes are over done; they are expensive, labor intensive, energy consuming and not always very attractive. Often retaining walls are covered with vegetation anyway so that you can't see them. What is the wall really holding? The soil could have been graded and the slope simply planted with erosion controlling vegetation.

Branch cuttings can be used as mulch, fuel, stakes and building supplies.

COMPOST PILES OR BINS

More sacrilege! Many customers ask me what they should do now that their compost pile is full and they are having difficulty turning it. Others have purchased compost bins that cost hundreds of dollars. If you want to make very high-quality soils for potting plants or starting seeds, it makes sense to spend the time and some money on a good system, but most people don't need this. Directly apply compost materials as mulch right where you are going to use it instead of composting.

 Making compost can be done in as few as 14 days and sometimes less.

REMOVAL OF ORGANIC MATERIALS

Natural organic materials are the basic foundation for future growth on your property. Don't let any of this leave your property. And, in the dark of night, go and get your neighbors' too that's been put out to the curb for pickup.

It's not necessary to till the whole garden when you can till limited areas.

You can grow raspberries, asparagus, apples and other perennial fruits and vegetables that don't require standard gardening methods.

ROTOTILLING

Many growers (farmers) have implemented no-till or low-till cultivation for their fields over the last three decades. There's no reason the American gardener should be stuck in the 1950s spending a lot of energy and time on tilling. Tilling compacts soils, brings weed seeds to the surface and damages tree roots. Just stop it!

GARDENING

The word "gardening" and many of its practices, like grubbing in the dirt on your hands and knees, will not be part of a sustainable landscape. Creating an eco-friendly yard may not include any traditional gardening methods if you are interested in low maintenance. Food plants normally grown in gardens can often be incorporated in no-till landscape beds.

Pet laying hens will clean up food scraps and produce high-quality finished compost fertilizer free for the gathering.

ORGANIC FERTILIZERS

There is no advantage to buying fertilizers made from corn, soybeans or human waste because there is a huge amount of energy that goes into creating and transporting these. Fish-emulsion fertilizer can be made from the waste of a sustainable fishery or just as easily from the rapidly disappearing species in our oceans. For free, you can harvest and use all of the surplus organic materials on your property and it will be a much more environmentally friendly fertilizer. See Removal of Organic Materials on page 19.

ADVICE FROM THE LOCAL GARDEN SHOP

Some garden shops actually have a person, or two, (take these people out to dinner) who might actually be able to help you. Most do not. An employee of a shop is not going to have the time to actually learn about your lifestyle in order to recommend what will fit your needs. Plan, at best, to get poor advice about plants. At worst, you end up buying something that wasn't right for you.

WHAT SOMEONE ELSE WANTS FOR YOU

What I want you to have, or what someone else wants for you, is a mistake. There are plenty of so called "experts" that just love to dictate to others, especially in the gardening world. Let them do what they want on their own property (it's surprising how little some of these people have actually accomplished for themselves). What is sustainable for others may not be sustainable for you. Your eco-friendly yard must be unique for your situation. If you want a landscape that will fit your lifestyle, then it's your wants and needs that have to be recognized — not anyone else's. If you need help, you can get assistance from a real expert that will work on your behalf, not his or hers.

NATIVE PLANTS

More blasphemy. Native plants make up at least 50 percent of the plants I sell, and my property is predominately native plants. However, you may not want native plants or your soil may be so changed that native plants won't do well. Some native plants are easy to grow, others are very difficult to establish. Many food plants are not native to where you live. When native-plant fanatics take me to task for how I feel, I suggest that we bring back all of the native animals too, like wolf packs running around the suburbs and bison grazing in the front yard. Usually, they will sulk away muttering what a nut I am!

There are many definitions of what a native plant is. Some think a native plant should be from a natural seed source that grows within 50 miles (80km) from where you live. Others think native refers to plants that at one time grew in your state or country.

A wet area of your property turns from a liability to a benefit when you grow something useful there, like wild rice.

Chapter 3
B.E.L.S.

Accomplish a sustainable landscape by taking advantage of four basic areas. Benefits, Efficiency, Lifestyle and Systems (B.E.L.S.) These areas will form the basic foundation for what you want to create.

BENEFITS

A landscape should not just be hard work, it should truly benefit you. Of course aesthetics are important, but what about all of the other things you can derive from a landscape? Each component of your landscape should offer multiple benefits.

My apple trees provide shade to sit in, fruit for eating, trimmings for mulch or fuel, nesting for birds and they look good too. When the tree dies, I turn the wood into fuel, make furniture, and use it to smoke fish and meats. I save a great deal of time because I don't apply pesticides to the trees and have

great pollination because beneficial insects are not harmed. Some apples turn out perfectly and the less than perfect ones are used for cooking. Does anyone care how an apple looked as long as the pie tastes good? For me, apple production is free and I get a lot of other benefits besides the apples. I spend less than two hours per year on each tree and that includes the time to pick a bushel of apples per tree.

My laying hens are also part of my landscape and they produce many benefits. They turn food waste, bugs, worms and weeds into all the fresh eggs we need. Sometimes, I trade eggs for freshly baked bread from my friend, Kerry. They also produce fertilizer for the garden, eat ticks that might carry disease, do a good job of weeding around my nursery plants so I don't have to and provide entertainment for visitors. The neighbors bring food scraps for them and love to take care of the chickens when we are away. Their benefit — they get to keep the farm fresh eggs. All this, and I only spend five minutes a day providing care for them.

EFFICIENCY

Your landscape, at this point, may be like a huge old locomotive demanding water, fuel and constant attention. You might feel that you are trapped shoveling coal endlessly just to keep it moving and you never catch up. The locomotive gobbles up the fuel as fast as you can throw it in. Now, picture your

An old wheelbarrow is transformed into a balanced wood carrier that only requires lifting strength of 15 pounds.

landscape as a huge solar generator that's just waiting for you to flip the switch — clean, quiet, cool and efficient.

Efficiency in landscapes is extremely important. Most homes have many energy features built in, but little thought is given to conservation in landscapes. In my climate, a quarter-acre (0.1ha) lot with sprinklers will use 80,000 gallons (3,028hl) of water a year just to try to grow grass. Yet, the house was built with low-flush toilets that only use 1.5 gallons (6L) per flush! Water, fuel, electricity, garbage removal, mining and transportation costs are just some of the things the average landscape uses that can make it very costly for the consumer and the environment. Your time might be the largest input if your landscape is inefficiently designed. The easiest gains in efficiency that you can make with your home and property are in retrofitting your landscape to use less resources and produce more benefits for you to use.

Benefits and efficiency are closely related. How much time, effort, money and energy you put into a landscape, and what you get in return, is important. If you don't reap enough benefits, it will be difficult for you to continue doing it. The more efficient you can be with installation and maintenance the more benefits you can derive from your landscape. Use this book to learn how to do some landscape jobs very rapidly using very few materials and create something of value to you.

If height scares you, my 120-foot (30m) wind tower that needs regular maintenance may not fit your lifestyle.

LIFESTYLE

Use your current lifestyle, or the lifestyle you want to achieve, as a foundation to create your eco-friendly yard. Lifestyle is probably the most over-looked part of a landscape design. You probably don't want to create a landscape that you don't like, but many people do this because they didn't analyze the lifestyle component. Everyone is different. What is your lifestyle? This question is easier to answer than you might think. Simply, what do you like or don't like? Make a list of your likes and dislikes using the following examples:

- I want a low-maintenance landscape because the kids keep me busy.
- I don't like to see any weeds because it looks messy.
- I want a quiet place to relax and unwind after work.
- I want a place to play with my pets rather than take them to the park.
- I would like to show others the neat things I can do in my landscape.
- I like the sound of water, but I don't want to do a lot of work.
- I want everything just right and I don't mind the extra work.
- I want to entertain my friends in my yard because I enjoy cooking.
- I want to grow some of my own food for health reasons.
- I like watching birds, but bird feeders are messy.
- I don't like bees because I'm allergic.
- I want a soccer field for the kids so I don't have to drive them somewhere else.

All of the above statements are things that can be integrated into your landscape. The key is to have them benefit how you want to live. By using the benefits and efficiency in the design, along with lifestyle, you can create a truly functional landscape.

Bare root trees can be part of an efficient system of planting during the dormant season.

SYSTEMS

Systems are ways of doing things in an established way. In general, landscapers are terrible at developing systems and homeowners trying to do a weekend project are even worse. I'm able to get more work done because I developed and use established systems in my office and at the work site. While every job is different, I use the same methods, tools and materials to achieve the desired effect. It's like an artist using the same brushes, canvas and paint to create wildly different results. Systems don't stifle my creativity; it allows me countless combinations to create landscapes that fit a lifestyle.

Systems of doing things are related to the benefits, efficiency and lifestyle. You probably already have systems for doing things in your landscape. Are benefits and efficiency part of your system? For instance, when trees are pruned, many people just stack up the branches or haul them out to the street. Instead, cut them up right away for fuel, stakes, furniture parts and mulch. Your tree-pruning system deals with correct pruning of trees and then finds uses for "waste" material that benefits you and results in you doing less work. I'll teach you how to do some of these things in the projects section.

A columnar buckthorn shrub
that needed to be removed
becomes fuel for my brick oven.

Chapter 4
Integrating Home and Landscape

Many people think that the landscape is an extension of the home — Wrong! Your home is an extension of your landscape. Good home design should consider the home from the outside in. Many people mistakenly design homes from the inside out without any regard to where or how the house is placed on the lot. The result is a home that functions poorly within its environment, is uncomfortable, and it's expensive to heat, cool and maintain. Your habitat is your entire property with everything that's a part of it. If you think of birds; they have a nest to raise their young, a place to roost, places to feed, a location for dust baths and another location to loaf. This may cover several acres, several square miles or even several countries. Although, you don't want your landscape to extend to several countries because air travel for non-avian species is such a hassle now. Each part of a bird's habitat is designed to optimize benefits, reduce stress and take full advantage of the natural environment.

Broadening the definition of home to include all of the habitat that you can use to your benefit is important. You can design your landscape to cool your home by shading, heat your home with waste wood produced on your property and provide outdoor entertainment areas that connect to compatible spaces in your home. In turn, your home structure can provide micro-climates to grow certain plants and roof water for irrigation.

INTEGRATING ENERGY

The easiest way to reduce energy needs for your home is through your landscape. Natural gas, electricity and fuel for your vehicle are not the only places to look for savings.

Grow your own food so you don't have to pay to transport it hundreds or thousands of miles. Peppers, tomatoes and other hot-climate plants do best right next to your house where it's hot and sunny. Expensive herbs easily can grow right outside the kitchen door for convenience. Tap into the run-off from your house roof to provide all of the free water you could ever use on your property. Rainwater is a great way to reduce the need and expense of city water, or the cost of pumping it. Make or convert a grill to cook food that burns wood scraps from your property — you won't have to

This pergola uses vines and shade cloth to cool a patio and a shop building.

purchase charcoal. Vines are an excellent way to shade south- and west-side windows in the warmer months. Perennial vines like hops, that die back to the ground at the end of the season, work very well for this. Taller evergreen trees and shrubs can significantly reduce heating costs of the home when used as a windbreak.

For northern climates, a passive solar sunroom attached to your home provides a place to start vegetable plants and it helps heat and cool your home. Covered porches in many climates provide a transition into the landscape and help protect and cool the house. An outdoor shower for use in warm weather can reduce cooling costs and humidity levels in the house. Outdoor entertainment and cooking areas help reduce costs because you stay at home rather than go out to eat, and it keeps your home cooler in warm weather.

Wide step units with at least 12-inch (30cm) treads and no more than a 6-inch (15cm) riser are most comfortable for outdoor use.

This copper fire bowl is supported by champagne bottles on end. Use a candle under the bowl to illuminate the bottles at night.

INTEGRATING STRUCTURES

You will enjoy your home and landscape more when they are properly integrated. Transitional areas like steps, walks, porches and decks are important elements. Recently, while working with a new customer, Janell, I watched as her husband, Chuck, hopped over the threshold of the patio door to a very narrow step that was eight inches (20cm) down to exit the house. It looked dangerous and uncomfortable to me. I showed them a new two-step unit that had wide steps that started at the level of the patio door and each step was only a six-inch (15cm) step down. They loved it! Now, it's comfortable and safe for them to step outside.

Based on your climate, you can create niches that appeal to you. We have a south-facing porch and patio for use early in the season when we want to sit and relax where it's a little sunnier and warmer. It's also a great area for stargazing. And when temperatures cool off during summer evenings, we're close to our fire pit. The sunroom on the south side provides places for people to sit who want to escape

Going from the house to outside areas should be like the experience of walking between rooms. Add soft lighting to the landscape so that nighttime use isn't any different outside than inside.

the bugs, yet still see the fire. We also have a north-facing porch and entertainment/cooking area that we use mid-to late summer when we want to take advantage of the shade provided by the house. Here, people who want some sun can sit on the patio and those that don't can move up to the shady porch and still participate in conversation.

Designated walkways and paths can be extremely helpful to show others the way and keep your favorite flowers from being trampled. A casual walkway of bark or pine needles is appropriate for lightly traveled areas. Places that get daily traffic would benefit from longer-lasting materials. For front walks and formal areas where there might be high-heel traffic, place good materials that don't have gaps, cracks or uneven surfaces so that you or your guests are not injured.

Make a path for your brick
oven using paver blocks.
No high heels allowed!

Chapter 5
Planning and Design

Planning and designing your eco-friendly yard and landscape requires 75 percent of your work. There is 24 percent for the maintenance and only one percent in the actual installation. Sounds strange doesn't it? Yet, couples plan a wedding two years in advance to get just the right place, the right food, the right people to enjoy it and the right gifts! And that's for an event that, at most, lasts a few hours. I'm assuming the marriage will last longer than that. Many people work extremely hard and spend many hours creating their landscape because they forgot about planning and design. The maintenance will be overwhelming because of that lack of planning too. An eco-friendly yard is all about the initial design and the maintenance that will occur, however small, for years to come. There are some landscapes that require no planting, installation or soil moving: just design and long-term management. This requires professional skills and years of experience to maintain the landscape as the customer desires.

Spend 100 hours thinking, planning and designing for each hour of working on a sustainable landscape.

THE PROPERTY OWNER QUESTIONNAIRE

A property owner questionnaire is perhaps the best way to start planning a sustainable landscape. If you are not discussing these questions with your landscaper, or asking yourself these questions before you begin working on your landscape, how will you know if you're getting the things you want in your landscape? The Property Owner Questionnaire is my way of marriage counseling. Years ago, I would visit potential customers at their home to discuss their new landscape. Do you want to know what I found out? In many cases, the couple **never** discussed this subject between themselves before I got there. The result — I became the conduit for great arguments between couples about who wanted what. I would sit and watch people shout at each other because neither had talked to the other before I got there about what the other was thinking. It wasn't long before I created a way for potential customers to channel their energy in a productive way. Arguments end rapidly (or at least when I'm there) when I tell them I have homework for them, hand them the Property Owner Questionnaire and tell them I won't work with them unless they complete it.

KEY TO THE QUESTIONNAIRE

PROPERTY INFORMATION

Property documentation is very important. Some of this information you may have received at the time of your property purchase. If you don't have a property survey, usually you can get one at an affordable price. Cutting down your neighbor's tree, or preparing your landscape on your neighbor's property, can end up costing you thousands of dollars. Surveys for many suburban lots may cost several hundred dollars. Knowing what you own and who regulates what you own is one of the basic things you need to know before making any changes to your property.

The items shown below are things that will assist you or your landscaper in preparing your design.

YES	NO	
☐	☐	Completed Property Owner Questionnaire
☐	☐	Property photos
☐	☐	Covenants
☐	☐	Certified survey
☐	☐	House plans
☐	☐	Site plan for construction
☐	☐	Septic system plan
☐	☐	Wetland, flood plain or ordinary high water-mark plan
☐	☐	Existing permits, compliance orders and/or enforcement actions
☐	☐	Communications that apply
☐	☐	Previous landscape plans

DECISION MAKERS

Who helps you make decisions? It might be quite a few people; others rely on themselves. Some of us don't like to make decisions but are willing to do the work once the decision is made. Others like to make decisions rapidly, while others need to gather as much information as possible to make sure they're making the right choice. In many cases, couples split up decisions based on how important something is to them or based on their expertise. Let's look at more questions from the Property Owner Questionnaire.

Please list below the partners making the decisions regarding the project.

_____   _____

(Please print name)   (Please print name)

☐   Financial decisions   ☐   Financial decisions

☐   Maintenance decisions   ☐   Maintenance decisions

☐   Design decisions   ☐   Design decisions

☐   Telephone contact   ☐   Telephone contact

BUDGETING

Failure to plan is planning for failure. Budgeting money, time and resources are all important to your success. I see many people build a house and then realize they have a mess because no thought was given to landscaping. What's worse, no budget for landscaping was set aside either. So, they seed a large area for a lawn because that is all they can afford at the moment. When the new grass burns off and dies because of lack of water, they buy a sprinkler system and re-seed. The grass starts growing thanks to being watered every day, but it turns yellow and is weedy. Now, they buy fertilizer and pesticides and pour them on. The grass grows like crazy and they have trouble keeping up because their mower is too small or old. They purchase a brand new riding mower to cut all that grass faster — the whole time watering and fertilizing even more. They end up cutting the grass twice a week and hate it.

At the end of five years, the family wonders how they could have spent $20,000 or $30,000 and end up with a lawn for a landscape, why their water bills are so high, why they don't have time to relax, why they are broke, and they still don't have the landscape that they really wanted. Then they call a professional and wonder how the situation can be changed, but "We don't have any money to do this." How aggravating! Break this cycle with budgeting.

Below is a worksheet to help you plan a budget so that you don't overspend and you spread out your expenses so that you can accomplish something every year. Some of you will laugh when you see some of the higher budget figures. However, if you have a friend or relative spending $50,000 a year on their landscape — give them my phone number!

BUDGETING WORKSHEET

INSTALLATION YEAR					YEAR/BUDGET AMOUNT
1st	2nd	3rd	4th	5th	
☐	☐	☐	☐	☐	$1,000 to $3,000
☐	☐	☐	☐	☐	$5,000
☐	☐	☐	☐	☐	$10,000
☐	☐	☐	☐	☐	$15,000
☐	☐	☐	☐	☐	$20,000
☐	☐	☐	☐	☐	$30,000
☐	☐	☐	☐	☐	$40,000
☐	☐	☐	☐	☐	$50,000 or more

DESIGN ANALYSIS

Review the following questions and make a list of all your preferences and how you plan to use your property. This is your opportunity as the user of the landscape to decide the different components and style of your desired landscape. Here are some excerpts from that section of the Property Owner Questionnaire.

OUR STYLE IS AS FOLLOWS:

YES	NO	
☐	☐	We prefer to have our landscape blend in with the adjoining landscapes.
☐	☐	We want our own unique landscape, but prefer that it be complemented by surrounding properties.
☐	☐	We want a landscape that stands out from the rest and defines ours as an outstanding property.
☐	☐	All plants should be clipped into formal shapes with a very neat and orderly emphasis.
☐	☐	Plants should grow together with a full blending of colors and textures.
☐	☐	Plants should have adequate spacing, but I prefer an informal feel.
☐	☐	Plants should be spaced far enough apart that they don't touch at all.
☐	☐	We enjoy a combination of both formal and informal plantings.

WE ENJOY THE FOLLOWING COLORS:

YES	NO		YES	NO	
☐	☐	Red	☐	☐	Orange
☐	☐	Burgundy	☐	☐	Yellow
☐	☐	Pink	☐	☐	Brown
☐	☐	Fuschia	☐	☐	Cream
☐	☐	Purple	☐	☐	White
☐	☐	Blue	☐	☐	Gray
☐	☐	Green	☐	☐	Black

THE FOLLOWING ACTIVITIES OCCUR ON OUR PROPERTY:

YES	NO		YES	NO	
☐	☐	Ball tossing	☐	☐	Bocce
☐	☐	Croquet	☐	☐	Horseback riding
☐	☐	Football	☐	☐	Reading
☐	☐	Baseball	☐	☐	Sunbathing
☐	☐	Soccer	☐	☐	Clothesline
☐	☐	Badminton/Volleyball	☐	☐	Swing set
☐	☐	Fly casting	☐	☐	Child's swimming pool
☐	☐	Golf swing practice	☐	☐	Clubhouse
☐	☐	Working on vehicles	☐	☐	Beach
☐	☐	Woodworking	☐	☐	Dock
☐	☐	Picnics and barbeques	☐	☐	Boating
☐	☐	Camp or cooking fire	☐	☐	Swimming pool
☐	☐	Debris and leaf burning	☐	☐	X-Country skiing
☐	☐	Dog run	☐	☐	Hiking

You can access all of the Property Owner Questionnaire, print it, and use it free of charge at www.landscapes4life.com.

CHOOSING A PLAN THAT'S RIGHT FOR YOU

After completing the Property Owner Questionnaire, you're ready to start on your plan or design. If you have adequate knowledge about landscaping you may feel comfortable doing the landscape yourself. However, most landscape designers, and all landscape architects, have at least a four-year college degree. To become a good designer, these individuals might have decades of on-the-ground experience. Throw in concepts of sustainability, where applied science is used to getting certain results, and the skill level needs to be even higher. Your neighbor who likes to "garden" is not going to be able to help you very much. Wherever you are located, you should be able to find a knowledgeable landscaper who can help you, and some experts will even help you from a distance. Use experts where and when you're able and rely on yourself for other areas.

Everyone sees things differently. I am a very visual person and like to plan right on-site. However, I can also read and visualize a plan on paper. You should pick the best way to design that works for you. A design or plan can be placed on paper to scale, it can be painted or flagged right on your yard or you can draw it on a photo. A plan is just that — a plan. It may not show you methods, conditions or how to accomplish what you want. A good addition to a plan is a written narrative that describes who, what, where, why and when. Often, committing to writing the progression of the project is something that you easily can do with your level of expertise. Sharing this narrative with an expert will fill in the blanks and offer suggestions.

A proliferation of consumer computer programs that help you design your own landscapes makes people think they are experts. Does a sharp pencil make someone an accountant? No! Save yourself some money and avoid the computer programs for design. Many of the features, including 3-D and "grow" to visualize your landscape, are misleading, and represent a design that will not meet your needs.

DESIGN — THE CONTINUAL PROCESS

Planning and design is an ongoing process. Your life changes, kids come and go, jobs change and interests expand. As you learn more things, you find that you have even more exciting options. As you find more options, you can add to your design. Design is all about having a place to start, exploring the process, making changes and growing your eco-friendly yard.

To help envision your plan, lay out a garden hose to provide the flowing lines right on your yard. This will help you delineate spaces and give you a feeling of scale.

Chapter 6

Tools That Work So You Don't Have To (or at least not as hard)

Perhaps one of the greatest difficulties for you to overcome in creating an eco-friendly yard is in tool use. Tool use and the methods for using these tools will make the difference between success and failure. I don't want to scare anyone with the types of tools that you really need to use to achieve results. However, you may never have heard of some of the tools let alone their use. Most gardening books want you to keep gardening; mindlessly puttering away with tools that don't fit your lifestyle. To attain a sustainable landscape, you'll want to avail yourself of tools that get the job done as rapidly and efficiently as possible.

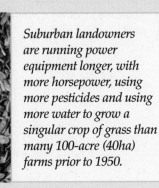

Suburban landowners are running power equipment longer, with more horsepower, using more pesticides and using more water to grow a singular crop of grass than many 100-acre (40ha) farms prior to 1950.

JUNK

Stores, garden centers, garages and tool sheds are full of tools for gardening and landscaping that are just junk. Poorly made, poorly designed, too much plastic, not enough good steel, too light or too heavy. There is a plethora of hand tools that require you to be on your hands and knees, which is a good way to spend your day not accomplishing anything. Poor quality tools are not only a waste of money, there are environmental costs too, in their production, shipping and disposal.

USING THE RIGHT TOOLS

You cannot find the quality of tools that you need for daily use at most department stores, garden centers and big box stores. Forget about what other people tell you to look for in design or materials. Do your own research on professional tool suppliers for landscapers, forestry professionals and agriculture. "You get what you pay for" has never been more appropriate than it is today in the purchase of landscape tools. The pruning shears that I have used every day for ten years is Swiss made, very comfortable, works well and will continue in service. They cost about $50 a pair now.

If you are right-handed and using pruning shears; use the left hand to lightly push the branch you are pruning. You can cut through a much larger branch when the blade of your pruning shears is cutting fibers under tension. Similar to cutting a rope that is pulled taut.

Less-costly shears can be had for $5 to $10 and will not work as well on their first cut as my old ones work on their 10,000 cut. And the cheap ones probably won't last a season.

You may think you don't need good tools because you won't use them very often. Not true! Because you don't do this all of the time, you are actually going to be harder on your tools than many professionals. Will that shovel handle hold up to being used as a pry bar? Will the blade of the saw get pinched in the cut and need some persuasion to get out? You get the idea. A quality tool will hold up to some abuse without breaking, can be fixed, sharpened and maintained.

Having the right tool for every job is nice, but sometimes you have to do with what you have. Many hand tools have multiple uses. You can use an edging spade to cut a "V" for edging, use it to cut a slit for wire placement for landscape lights, and use it to wedge between paver bricks to straighten and align them. A flexible leaf rake can be used, yes, to rake leaves, skim string algae off small ponds, and the tines can hold marshmallows or hotdogs for roasting.

BETTER AND FASTER

There are two ways to be more efficient with your tools. The first way is to not have to use them to start with. As an example, cut off trees and shrubs flush with the ground and don't dig the root systems out. The second way to be more efficient is to use the right tool for the least amount of time. Too many gardening books show you the hard way of doing things. The average person cannot make a substantial change to their landscape with just a shovel and a wheelbarrow.

I recall a customer who had their college student home for the summer, and instead of a paying job, the student spent the whole summer digging out an area for a patio and moving the soil to a pile in the yard and then using a wheelbarrow to haul in the gravel. The customer was quite surprised when I mentioned, contrary to the department store landscape book that he had, that since there was such sandy soil in this location the paver material could have been laid directly on the sand and the excavation wasn't needed. Not to mention that a small machine could have done in four hours what this student spent hundreds of hours doing. What did this kid learn?

HIGH TECH REALLY MATTERS

Where would people be without their cell phones, PDAs and computers? The truth is, most people haven't kept up with the truly high-tech tools that are making their lives and others lives easier every day. Growing up in the early 1960s, if we didn't build it, grow it or fix it, we didn't have it. The tools we had to make this happen where rudimentary at best. Over the last thirty years, there have been so many good tools developed or highly refined, but very few people know how to use them for sustainable landscapes, or even know that they exist.

Some of these tools are:

- The mulching lawn mower is probably a tool that you already have. Yes, these are great for leaving the clippings on you lawn. You also can use these for mowing down and mulching up smaller perennials and ground cover plants at the end of the season. This is a quick and neat way of mulching.
- Powered hedge trimmers are another standard yard maintenance tool that you probably already have. You can grow certain shrubs in your landscape just for mulch production. The hedge trimmers let you rapidly and efficiently cut up these plants for mulch. It's also a fast way to deadhead your larger perennials producing even more mulch in place.
- Modern chain saws with safety features, but quite possibly the most dangerous tool you will ever use, are a fast way to cut up woody debris for a variety of uses.
- Weed whips and/or string trimmers are very useful and fast in a sustainable landscape to take out weeds or mulch plant material.
- Power brush saws are used for cutting down shrubs and woody weeds. It is very powerful, easy-to-use and extremely safe to use since you are harnessed and can't get near the blade.

Leaving your clippings on your lawn over one season can eliminate one fertilizer application because the nutrients in the clippings get recycled. By leaving the clippings of perennials in place, your gardens will not need additional mulch.

Torches for burning off weeds only remove the top of the weed. This is a slow and potentially dangerous way of getting rid of weeds. Weed whips do the same job much faster and with less effort.

You can rent a mini-skid steer and learn to operate it well in a few hours. Backhoe attachment (shown), auger, pallet fork and buckets are just a few of the attachments.

- Sickle mowers/brush mowers are easy to use and a great way to harvest mulch or mulch in place. I use our sickle mower to harvest the cattails at the edge of our pond for mulch and to keep the cattails from spreading over the entire area.
- Mini-skid steers can replace your shovel and wheelbarrow. It is not the big skid steer that you sit in. You either stand on or walk behind these powerful machines. A single skilled operator with a mini-skid steer will do the work of a landscape crew of six with shovels and wheelbarrows.

LESS IS MORE

Many of the tools used for maintaining standard landscapes are run for hours at a time. Almost everyone I know has a story about a neighbor who is constantly running lawn equipment on their city or suburban lot, which is why some cities have put limits on when equipment can be run. It would have been better if they just required people to get a life! In sustainable landscapes, you only have to run power equipment for a short period of time to accomplish tasks. On the seven and one-half acres (3ha) of property where I have my home and nursery, I run less power equipment than people who have quarter-acre (0.1ha) lots. Smaller lawn areas mean you run the mower less. No-till gardens mean that you'll only have to mulch up plant material at the end of the season instead of repeatedly running a rototiller. Because you can directly mulch leaves and branches, there is no need for a noisy chipper. Letting pine needles build up under pines where grass won't grow anyway significantly reduces the use of a power blower or yard vacuum. A well-designed yard means that you won't need to use a string trimmer after mowing because obstacles were eliminated.

Using tools and equipment less can be better for your health and your tools will last longer too.

Most homeowner-grade power equipment is designed to run about 45 minutes at a time. Running it longer shortens its life expectancy since they are not designed for constant use and high temperatures.

Studies show that being in nature improves health, protects from illness, reduces stress and speeds up recovery after a hospitalization.

Chapter 7

Personality Approach to a Lifestyle Landscape

WHAT'S YOUR LIFESTYLE?

Who manufactured your car? Who built your computer? What credit card do you use? Whose name is printed on your running shoes? I'll bet you know the answer to these questions. These brand names are often associated with fun, power, style, ruggedness and success to name a few.

So what about your lifestyle brand? You're going to work, taking care of the kids, paying the bills and pretending to listen when your spouse talks to you. Are you doing something fun every day? Are you doing things that positively benefit your health? Are you developing meaningful routines to last a lifetime? Do you feel in control and at peace? Can you sum up your lifestyle in a sentence or two?

Things that bring meaning and focus to many people's lives are often found in nature. Why is nature so important to most people that they often have pictures or paintings at work and at home of mountains, waterfalls, birds, butterflies and lush greenery? Do pictures take the place of nature? **Absolutely NOT!**

There are many studies about the positive benefits to spending time immersed in nature for children and adults. Are you spending at least a little time outdoors in nature everyday? Being out on the golf course or walking a paved road or sidewalk does not count. Why would you confuse heavily maintained turf and man-made materials with nature?

Reusing and recycling can be part of anyone's sustainable lifestyle.

Our chickens serve many purposes and help keep us in touch with where our food comes from.

Living your lifestyle brand has benefits for you and the environment. Do you define part of who you are as concerned about global warming, interested in a green lifestyle, an avid recycler, and a person who wants to make a difference?

On our property, we have an outdoor brick oven that I use almost daily during the summer, quiet places to reflect, trails for walking, an outdoor shower for warm weather use and even a place for a few laying hens for fresh eggs! Our property also provides some easy-to-harvest foods, firewood to heat our home and places to relax at the end of our workday. Why go on vacation when every day can be a vacation? Not only do we achieve the kind of lifestyle that many people dream about, but there are also financial rewards. We save hundreds of dollars a year just in gas for the car because we are not running to the store for every little thing or going out to eat as much.

Things that you can add to your own property to help you achieve your lifestyle may include:

- Trees, shrubs and other plants that provide homes for wildlife.
- Features built into your property to use and conserve rainwater.
- Easy-to-grow edible plants.
- Places for unstructured play and observing nature for kids and adults.
- Quiet places on your property to rest and get away from it all.
- Fun places to entertain friends and "eat out."

You get to decide. Is your lifestyle brand tattered and frayed by the stress of having to jump in the car and battle traffic for everything you want to do? Or, will you choose to take advantage of what is right outside your door with all of the benefits of health, confidence and hassle-free living?

Sustainable Lifestyle Pyramid

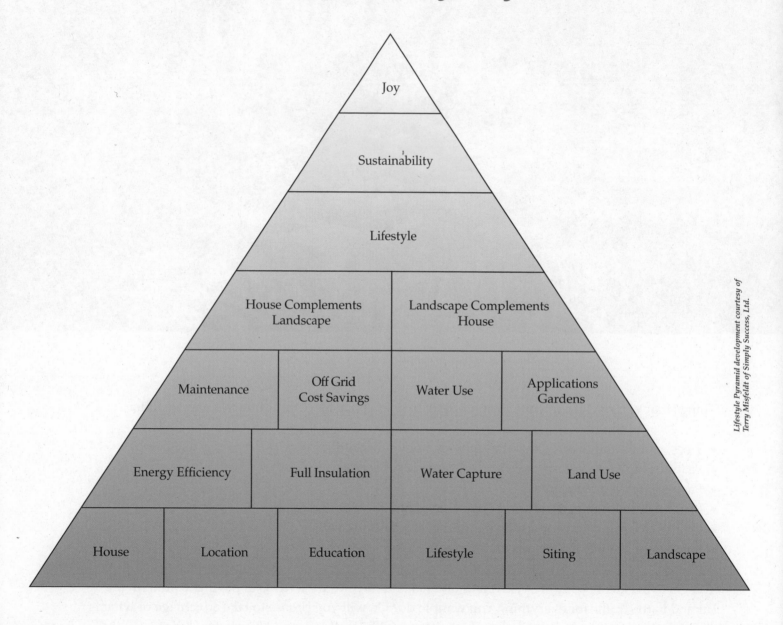

Joy

Sustainability

Lifestyle

House Complements Landscape | Landscape Complements House

Maintenance | Off Grid Cost Savings | Water Use | Applications Gardens

Energy Efficiency | Full Insulation | Water Capture | Land Use

House | Location | Education | Lifestyle | Siting | Landscape

Lifestyle Pyramid development courtesy of Terry Misfeldt of Simply Success, Ltd.

USING THE SUSTAINABLE LIFESTYLE PYRAMID

This Sustainable Lifestyle Pyramid serves as an outline for you as a property owner to make the utmost use of your piece of ground. It encompasses desired lifestyle, energy efficiency, environmental awareness, ecological care, and long-term sustainability.

At the base of the Sustainable Lifestyle Pyramid are the two cornerstones for a property intended to be a homestead: House and Landscape. You live in your home — your property should complement that home, provide sustainability options, and serve as a destination that matches your lifestyle.

Next to the cornerstones are the critically important factors of Siting and Location. Location is a major factor for the landscape because it involves where the property is situated. Is it in an urban or rural location? Siting studies the piece of land for solar, wind, soil, drainage, and other factors to determine the best place to put the house. Obviously, lot lines and ordinances are considerations too.

Where someone chooses to purchase their piece of property determines what they will be able to do with it, which is why Education is part of the foundation. Potential and existing homeowners need to learn about the possibilities for a place where they will spend a majority of their lives when they're not at work, and maybe their property will be where they work. If quiet, peaceful sleep is important, it will be important to look for property away from busy, major interstate highways. Likewise, if being close to work or social activity is an important variable, a country estate may not be the most viable choice. Having a home-based business could mean access to high-speed Internet connections and other amenities, such as parking space for customers, which then become determining factors in location and siting.

Lifestyle becomes a consideration at the basic level because property owners who want to raise chickens may encounter problems with municipal ordinances. Having fruit-bearing trees on the property can provide a sustainable source of food while adding to the aesthetic beauty of the land. Lifestyle considerations include factors, such as, do you like to entertain, enjoy a peaceful retreat, do you want a showcase in the neighborhood, or is it essential to have gardens where you can work on raising hybrid flowers or a productive vegetable crop?

At the next level of the Sustainable Lifestyle Pyramid are two factors influencing the sustainability of the house and two factors impacting the landscape. Energy Efficiency involves looking at options, such as earth sheltering, the heating source in northern climates, windows, shading, passive-solar applications and numerous other choices. Houses need to breathe; yet the building needs to be thoroughly insulated to prevent heat loss in winter and cooling loss in summer. Making the right choices at the beginning of the process may mean a more significant outlay at first, but the long-term benefits for a sustainable, low-maintenance, high-efficiency lifestyle far outweigh the initial investment.

On the property side of the pyramid, Water Capture and Land Use involve wise use of natural resources available through proper landscaping. When rain falls, it needs to go somewhere. Most modern landscapes channel the water away from the home, across the lawn, and into the storm sewer or drainage ditch … where it is lost to the homeowner. Water can be diverted to cisterns, ponds, or swales where it can be used as non-potable water for irrigation and a multitude of other applications with proper landscaping.

Determining how the land will be used can make the maximum use of every aspect of the property to sustain your desired lifestyle. Open treeless areas can be good locations for solar panels or garden beds. Mature tree stands can provide scrap firewood for brick ovens, fireplaces or masonry heaters. Often, it's merely a process of thinking through every potential use and then determining which are most feasible to fit your preferred lifestyle.

As we move further up the Sustainable Lifestyle Pyramid, we look at factors such as Maintenance. If you want to minimize the work involved in maintaining your home and land, options, such as a steel roof are considered, as are prairie grasses and other alternatives to gravel mulches and lawns. To reduce reliance on energy from utility companies, increased insulation choices are complemented by wind, solar, and other passive alternative energy sources. On the landscape side, how the captured water is to be used becomes a consideration, such as outdoor showers and drip irrigation systems. We also consider the different applications available to the property owner, such as fruit tree orchards, vineyards, vegetable gardens, domesticated animal habitats (chicken coops, dog runs, rabbit hutches, etc.), and countless other options.

As the foundation fills in and the Sustainable Lifestyle Pyramid grows, efforts are directed at making sure the house and home complement the various aspects of the property and landscape. A perfect example would be having an herb garden cultivated close to the kitchen preparation area. The landscape should also complement the house, such as providing shade on the house in the morning or afternoon to reduce energy consumption on hot summer days.

When these elements come together, you achieve the lifestyle that is desired and a destination you can enjoy for a lifetime. You'll also be able to sustain that lifestyle in a highly efficient, low-maintenance, and cost-effective manner for years. That is the epitome of a sustainable lifestyle.

Your lifestyle helps decide what features will function best for your landscape. Your personality helps decide how the finished design of these features will feel and look.

When your landscape is designed with input from your lifestyle and personality, it all fits together and makes it a sustainable design. You may have taken a personality test as part of a class or exercise at work and not been impressed. Were you a certain color, shape or animal? These sorts of classifications are hard to remember and even harder to relate to. We've simplified the personality groups to make this easier and I think you will find yourself with one or two of the basic personalities that we discuss.

THE BASIC FOUR

My friend, Terry, helped me understand the basic four personalities and how to work with them and how they relate to landscapes. These four basic personalities that reveal themselves in landscapes are:

- Bold
- Fun
- Perfectionist
- Easy-going

You can have all four of these personalities, however, one or two will be stronger than the rest. If your spouse or partner has a strong personality that is different than yours, that's OK. Different personalities can show themselves in different ways in the landscape and often complement each other. As soon as you understand these different personalities, the arguments over what goes in the landscape nearly disappear. You learn what and why you want it, and you realize why others have their own choices.

Lifestyle is what you do or what you would like to do. Personality is how you do it or how you would be most comfortable doing it.

Chapter 8
The Bold Personality

I used to think that people who exhibited a bold personality were kind of "show offs." Well guess what? They are, and that's not a problem. Before I recognized this trait, customers approached me with very grand plans, fountains and ponds in the front yard and oversized landscape features. I was befuddled. I didn't understand why someone would want a pond in the front yard when I like them in the back where there is more privacy. If you have a bold personality, you like to show what you can do, but you also love sharing what you have done with others. You want others to see it and you take pride in what you have accomplished.

Bold personalities tend to be extroverts, like their questions answered immediately, and they often rapidly make up their minds once information has been provided. I have found I need to offer options to this group. In sustainable landscapes, bold personalities can excel for being the first to bring new technologies to their area. Bold personalities are comfortable and open to new ideas but want to control the outcome.

There are things that can cause bold personalities problems. Building too big can be an issue if you have this personality. To avoid this problem, a budget should be prepared ahead of time to look at the initial cost, cost overrun areas, long-term maintenance costs and future energy costs. I had a customer who wanted to have a large, showy waterfall installed with a great deal of water being pumped to simulate the falls. I determined running that type of pump would cost about five dollars per day and was concerned about that expense. It turned out the customer was too. He settled on a much smaller pump that used only fifty cents per day in electricity, but we carefully constructed the falls to take full advantage of the water we were pumping. Now, he wants to be able to turn the volume of water down lower when guests visit so that conversation near the waterfall is not drowned out.

If you have a bold personality, I think you will enjoy showing what you can do with the projects in the following chapter. These tend to be a little more difficult than other projects, and paying attention to the details is important. Others will be impressed by the control you have over your landscape when you implement these projects.

To get the most out of an artificial waterfall made from natural stone, set the stones in insulating foam dispensed from a can. The foam seals the stones so most of the water flows over the top.

Solar electric fencer on movable chicken cage to protect young chicks from predators.

PROJECTS FOR BOLD PERSONALITIES
Solar Electric Fence

Solar panels in your landscape make a statement. They are very visible, and others are sure to ask you questions about them. We use them in our landscape because they do not require running new electric lines and we have the option of easily moving them. Solar panels vary by wattage and your supplier can help you fit the right panel for your project. These panels are independent of the power utility and will operate even when a storm takes out the power in the neighborhood. Your lights can be on when your neighbors aren't!

Our solar electric fence unit is the least costly of the solar panels and is fast and easy to hook-up. We have used these to protect our nursery plants from deer and protect our chickens from predators. You also can use a solar electric fence to control what is trying to eat your favorite landscape plants. Animals (and people) that touch the fence will receive a non-life-threatening shock. We have been occasionally amused when children that won't take "no" for an answer, grab the charged fence anyway. We surmise that this may be the only way for some children to get an immediate reprisal for doing something they were told not to do. Solar fence chargers are not as strong as plug-in ones that will actually kill weeds that come in contact with the fence.

Solar fence chargers can be attached to a standard electric fence or electric fence tape that has wire filaments in it and is more visible. Peanut butter can be applied to metal paddles that hang from the fence or applied directly to the tape. This will entice deer to experience the fence so that they will avoid it. Deer hair and hide may be too thick to get much of a shock, so tongue and nose make a better impression.

When the sun is present, the unit stores up electricity in a rechargeable battery that is self-contained. At night, or on cloudy days, the battery will continue to charge the fence. Solar-powered electric fence units usually come with complete instructions. Additional materials will be available where you buy your unit.

SUPPLIES

Solar electric fence unit
Ground rod
Ground rod clamp
Fence posts
Insulated wire holders
  for fence posts
Electric fence wire or
  electric fence tape
Screws or nails

TOOLS

Hammer
Pliers
Posthole digger or post
  pounder to install the posts
Wrench or pliers for
  lugs and clamps
Screwdrivers

Solar powered units can be mounted on a fence, post or structure.

Solar electric fence on chicken house deters predators from entering.

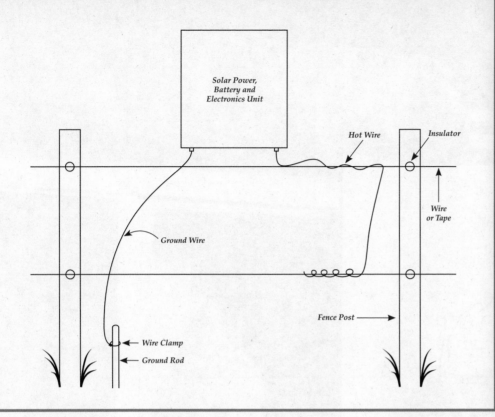

Solar Power,
Battery and
Electronics Unit

Hot Wire

Insulator

Wire
or Tape

Ground Wire

Fence Post

Wire Clamp

Ground Rod

Typical wiring diagram for
solar electric fence unit.

STEP-BY-STEP INSTRUCTIONS

1. Mount unit on post or wall in desired location using holes
provided for screws or nails with the solar panel facing the sun.
2. Pound in the ground rod near the unit.
3. Attach wire to ground lug on panel and clamp to ground rod.
4. Attach fence wire to power lug and run it to the fence location.
5. Twist wire from power lug onto fence wire.
6. Turn on the power switch to the unit and you are done.

*Electric fence wire or tape
needs to be insulated or
attached to an insulated
fastener wherever it
touches a fence post. If
the wire is in contact
with soil, weeds or tree
limbs, there will be less
or no shock distributed.*

Solar Panel for Lighting and Pumps

The medium-sized second panel is used to charge a battery that will provide lighting for the chicken house a few hours a night during the winter. Chickens need about 14 hours of light per day to lay eggs, so it's necessary to supplement sunlight to get eggs. You can use a solar panel like the one shown to provide power for a shed light, sign light, security light, house address numbers, and for a statue, fountain or waterfall. This setup is also used for a 12-volt water pump to supply the outdoor shower. Follow the manufacturer's directions for the units you purchase. Wire size and length depends on what you are powering. The manufacturer of the parts you purchase will provide wire gauge/length calculations.

SUPPLIES

Solar panel of
  appropriate size
Deep-cell battery (just
  borrow your neighbor's
  trolling motor battery)
Battery box
Proper size of 12-volt,
  2-strand wire
Solar controller unit
Timer unit
Wire nuts
Staple gun
Wire staples
Battery terminal connectors
12-volt outdoor
  lights, if desired
12-volt RV water
  pump, if desired
12-volt to 110-volt
  inverter, if desired
Fuse holders and fuses
Switches as needed

TOOLS

Wire strippers/crimpers
Screwdrivers
Wire cutters
Hammer

This solar panel was mounted using an angle bracket from the hardware store and standard nuts, bolts and screws.

You can injure yourself with solar panels and batteries. Solar panels can cause shocks, burns and fires. Batteries can explode, leak acid and cause fires. Follow all manufacturer's recommendations for use, safety, proper wiring and use of fuses. Fuses on solar powered equipment and batteries provide similar protection as house and auto fuses. Make sure to use the proper size fuses and wiring as recommended by the manufacturer of your equipment. A licensed electrician can help you with all your solar wiring needs and may be required in some areas.

STEP-BY-STEP INSTRUCTIONS

1. Mount solar panel facing the sun.
2. Run 12-volt wire to battery/controller/timer as specified by the manufacturer.
3. Run wire from the timer to desired light fixtures. Or, run wire from the battery to pump or other fixtures not on the timer.
4. Strip wires as needed.
5. Attach wires to solar panel per manufacturer's directions.
6. Place fuse holders and fuses as required by manufacturer.
7. Place switches as needed.
8. Staple wires to secure them.
9. Place battery in battery box and secure per manufacturer's instructions.

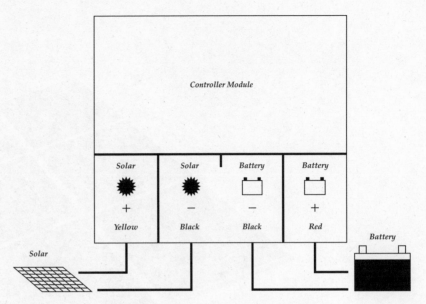

Controller Module

Solar	Solar	Battery	Battery
+	−	−	+
Yellow	Black	Black	Red

Solar

Battery

Typical 12-volt controller wiring diagram.

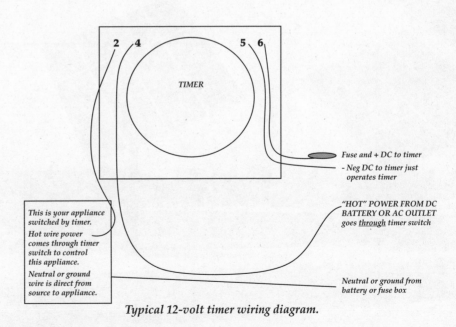

2 4   5 6

TIMER

Fuse and + DC to timer

- Neg DC to timer just
  operates timer

This is your appliance
switched by timer.

Hot wire power
comes through timer
switch to control
this appliance.

Neutral or ground
wire is direct from
source to appliance.

"HOT" POWER FROM DC
BATTERY OR AC OUTLET
goes <u>through</u> timer switch

Neutral or ground from
battery or fuse box

Typical 12-volt timer wiring diagram.

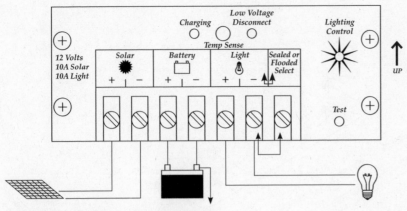

Controller for lighting system on page 77.

Large Solar Panel

Each one of our solar panels has a different task. We like the idea of keeping our solar panels separated so that if there is a problem, it only affects one system.

   The large solar panel that we have is used to power our outdoor lights. Large panels like these can be linked together to provide large amounts of power. You could power your entire house, a cabin, a shop, use for emergency power generation or power pumps, fans and motors. You can even sell power back to the utility company in some areas using panels like these. However, there is a cost to these panels. The large panel, page 75, shown costs about $600 and should last at least 20 years. You may need five or 10 of these panels to power an entire home. The panel and components should all work together. When you purchase the panel(s), you can also get directions for the other components.

   Our panel stores electricity in a rechargeable battery. A controller monitors the battery charge, acts as a timer, and uses the panel as a photo-eye to turn on the lights when the sun goes down and turn off the lights when desired. I'm very impressed with the controller we have for this panel. It is about the size of a cell phone, performs all of the functions properly, is rugged, well-labeled for wire placement and it's waterproof. It is one of the easiest products to wire and use that I have seen.

SUPPLIES

Solar electric panel (size and wattage
   determined by application)
Mounting track for panel
   and hardware
Mounting pole per manufacturer
Ground rod
Ground clamp
12-volt, 2-strand wire
   per manufacturer
Wire nuts
12-volt deep-cell battery/batteries
12-volt fuses
12-volt fuse holder
Battery connectors
Controller
12-volt to 110-volt inverter, if you
   want to operate 110-volt products
Vault or box for components
   (I used an irrigation vault)
Lights or other fixtures as desired

TOOLS

Posthole digger
Sledgehammer
Wrenches
Screwdrivers
Wire stripper/crimper
Pliers
Shovel
Drill
Drill bits

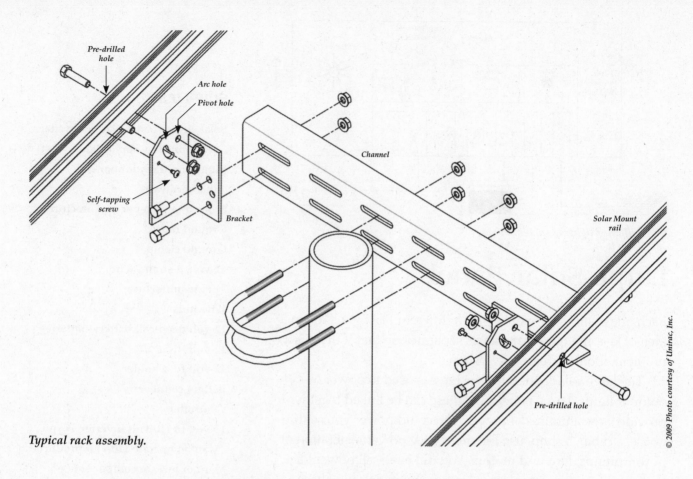

Pre-drilled
hole

Arc hole

Pivot hole

Self-tapping
screw

Bracket

Channel

Solar Mount
rail

Pre-drilled hole

Typical rack assembly.

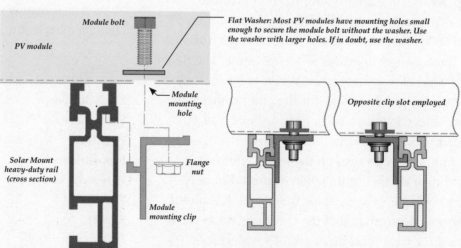

Module bolt

PV module

*Flat Washer: Most PV modules have mounting holes small
enough to secure the module bolt without the washer. Use
the washer with larger holes. If in doubt, use the washer.*

Module
mounting
hole

Opposite clip slot employed

Solar Mount
heavy-duty rail
(cross section)

Flange
nut

Module
mounting clip

Typical attachment of rack to panel.

In spring of 2008, a lightning strike nearby destroyed most of the LED lights that were attached to our panel. LEDs are very susceptible to electrical spikes and even static electricity. At this time, I would advise using LEDs cautiously. Solar panels and the associated electronics can also be damaged by lightning.

STEP-BY-STEP INSTRUCTIONS

1. Assemble rack per PV panel manufacturer's directions.
2. Attach rack to PV panel per manufacturer's instructions.
3. Pound in ground rod and follow manufacturer's directions for grounding.
4. Install vault or box to hold battery and electronics.
5. Follow recommendations for wiring controller and battery.
6. Install fuse holders and fuses on wiring per manufacturer.
7. Install your choice of fixtures.
8. Get ready to answer questions from your neighbors.

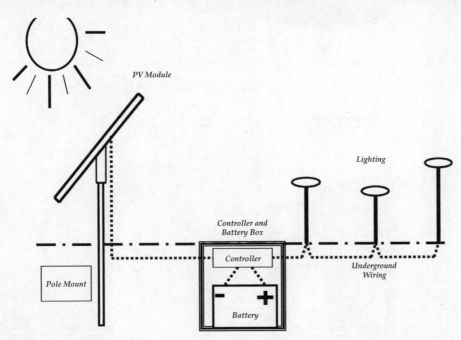

PV Module

Lighting

Controller and
Battery Box

Controller

Pole Mount

Underground
Wiring

Battery

Twelve-volt lighting system.

Wire nuts are used for connecting wire and you can find them in various sizes and numbers of wire. You may need several sizes. Wire is stripped to a prescribed length and the wire nuts are twisted on.

For outdoor use, there are wire nuts and other connectors that contain gels or a sealant so the connection or wires do not corrode. You may be required to use a certain type in your area. For most outdoor low-voltage wiring, we use standard wire nuts that we fill with 100-percent silicone caulk and then insert the wires to provide a waterproof connection.

Remember to check the level of electrolyte in the battery cells every two months. Charging of the battery causes loss of water. To refill, use clean water and only fill to the lower ring (about ½" (1.25cm) down) from the capped opening. Each cell of the battery needs to be checked and filled accordingly. If you see a metal grid above the liquid level in the battery, electrolyte level is very low and battery damage can result.

Micro-Irrigation

You may have pop-up sprinklers because you like the look of a nice lawn to complement your home. But are your sprinklers properly watering your perennials and ground covers that also showcase your home? Micro-irrigation is a way of watering that uses less water and allows you to control where the water goes. You can rapidly install micro-irrigation to help plants look their best and you can save money and have healthier plants by targeting your water application. Your friends and neighbors won't believe how good your landscape looks when you use a watering system like this, and you'll grow enormous fruits and vegetables.

Pop-up sprinklers are designed for watering turf and often do not do a good job of watering planting beds. Small sprinkler heads on legs do a great job of watering and look good too. These small sprinkler heads can be installed so your house walls or sidewalks don't get wet too. Remember, you get to decide where the water goes.

The micro-irrigation kit with garden hose fittings can be hooked to your outdoor faucet, or a fitting can be put on your existing irrigation system to provide water.

STEP-BY-STEP INSTRUCTIONS

1. Do not cut tape or straps on coil of irrigation line until step 8.
2. Locate the end of the irrigation line that is on the outside of the roll.
3. Wiggle on barbed fitting.
4. Secure with hose clamp.
5. Put Teflon® tape or compound on male pipe threads of barbed fitting.
6. Thread female garden hose fitting on male pipe threads of barbed fitting.
7. Attach female garden hose fitting to garden hose, faucet or fitting on existing irrigation system.

SUPPLIES

¾" (2cm) or 1" (2.5cm) irrigation line
Hose clamps
Male garden hose fittings with female pipe thread
Female garden hose fittings with female pipe thread
Female garden hose thread end caps
Barb fittings with male pipe thread
Teflon tape or pipe thread compound
Erosion fabric metal staples
Mizzle Wizard® sprinkler heads or similar item

TOOLS

Shears or saw to cut plastic tubing
Drill and bits
Screwdrivers
Adjustable wrench or pliers

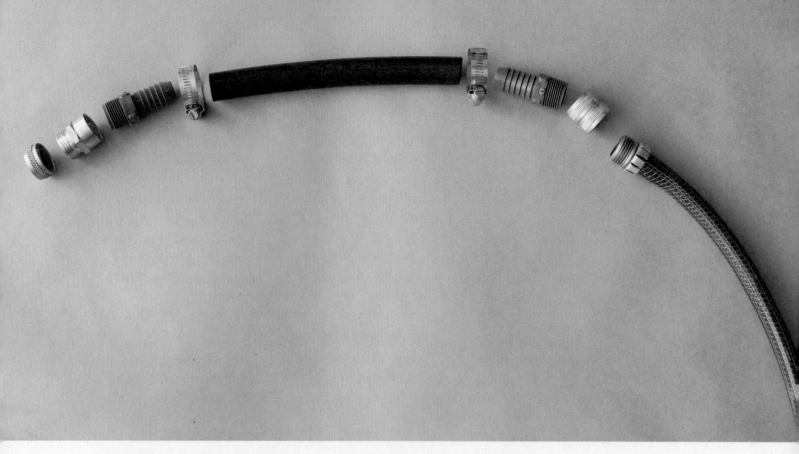

Sample section of irrigation line and fittings prior to installation. The coil of irrigation line you buy will be at least 100 feet (30m) long and can be cut to the length that you want.

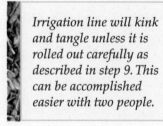
Irrigation line will kink and tangle unless it is rolled out carefully as described in step 9. This can be accomplished easier with two people.

8. Cut tape or straps that hold the coil of irrigation line.
9. Carefully roll out irrigation line from the coil like you would roll a spare tire for a car.
10. Place staples over hose to hold it down or use rocks, bricks or heavy tools.

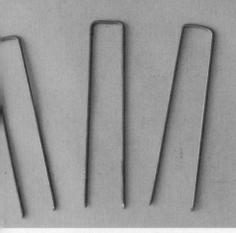 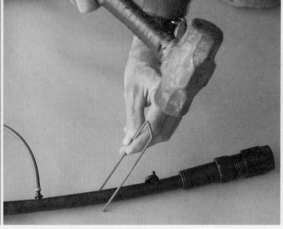 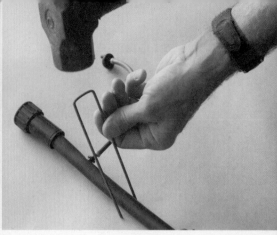

Purchase staples like these from a landscape supplier or landscaper in your area.

Place staples around irrigation line. For loose soil, secure the line with two staples at opposing angles next to each other.

11. Carefully, continue rolling out irrigation line and installing staples until you have completed the area.

12. Spacing of the irrigation line will depend on how far apart you want the Mizzle Wizard heads that have a seven-foot diameter spray.

13. When using other types of sprinkler heads, check size of spray diameter to determine spacing.

14. Wiggle on barbed fitting to end of irrigation line.

15. Secure with hose clamp.

16. Put Teflon tape or compound on male pipe threads of barbed fitting.

17. Thread male hose fitting on male pipe threads of barbed fitting.

18. Thread end cap on male garden hose fitting.

 *Let coil of irrigation line sit in the sun for awhile on cool days to make it more pliable.*

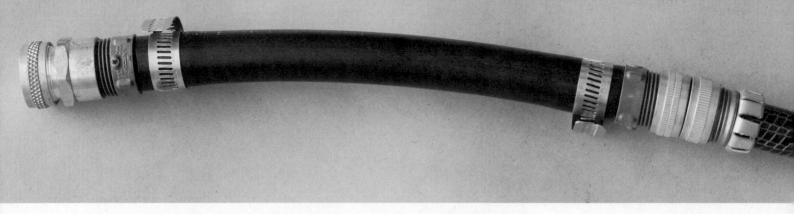

This hose has all of the fittings properly installed with the garden hose attached.

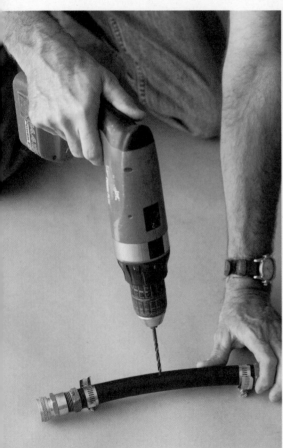

Drill carefully with slight pressure to avoid going all of the way through the line.

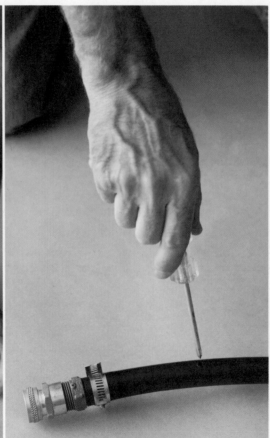

The hole will have a sharp edge after drilling. Slightly beveling the hole will help when inserting the line from the Mizzle Wizard.

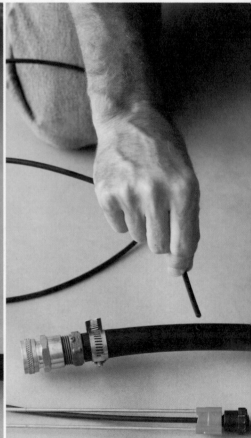

Soak the Mizzle Wizard hose in ice water to make it stiffer and easier to install.

Hide the irrigation line with mulch since burying is not necessary.

Because water pressure drops with the addition of each head, it is necessary to test each time a new head is placed. Additional heads may need to be closer together to reach the desired spray coverage.

19. Pick the location of your first Mizzle Wizard or similar sprinkler head.

20. Using the drill bit recommended by the manufacturer, drill a hole through one wall of the irrigation line.

21. Enlarge and bevel the hole slightly with a Phillips screwdriver.

22. Slide small hose of Mizzle Wizard into hole on the hose.

23. Friction and water pressure hold the hose in place. No other fittings are necessary unless you are using a different type of sprinkler head.

24. Place Mizzle Wizard by pushing the metal legs into the soil.

25. Turn on water and check diameter of spray.

26. Repeat steps 19 to 25 for each head installed.

27. Adjust sprinkler heads by moving them around or adjusting the height.

28. Finish by covering irrigation line with mulch or burying if you prefer.

Advanced Entertainment Areas

An advanced entertainment area can be the showcase of your property. Imagine how impressed your friends will be with the amenities and the types of food that you can prepare outdoors.

MUST HAVE ITEMS

To entertain in style, consider a patio or deck, cooking facilities, seating, and appropriate vegetation to create this outdoor room. You can do parts of the building for an advanced entertainment area yourself, but you may need professional assistance to achieve the desired results.

STEPS TO ACHIEVE YOUR ADVANCED ENTERTAINMENT AREA

1. Determine number of guests to create the right sized area.
2. Determine features that are most important to you.
3. Assemble preliminary estimates for features.
4. Create a budget and stick with it.
5. Create a plan for the entire area using a landscape designer or landscape architect so that it will look right and function properly.
6. Chose appropriate materials for all construction.
7. Apply for any needed permits.
8. Hire the necessary help that you need including landscapers, masons, electricians and plumbers.
9. Familiarize yourself with maintenance and operator instructions for all new features and appliances.
10. Invite your friends over and really impress them!

In cold climates, you can build a wood-fired brick oven for about $10,000 that will hold up to the weather. In warm climates, it may be possible to build a working oven for much less.

Brick Oven

If you are serious about cooking food that will "Wow" everyone and it's literally one of the hottest ways of preparing dinner, you'll want a wood-fired brick oven like the one shown.

Traditional wood-fired brick ovens were, and still are, designed to burn wood directly in the oven. If you want pizza, the coals are pushed to the back of the oven and you cook the pizza directly on the hearth. If you are baking breads, the ashes are removed, the temperature allowed to settle, and you cook directly in the oven. If you like steak and shrimp, a cast-iron griddle can be heated in the oven while there are still flames. After the cast-iron is hot, it can be removed from the oven, food placed on the hot griddle (do you hear sizzling yet?) and the steak or seafood can be cooked outside of the oven. (Food must be a thinner slice.) Or, the cast-iron griddle can be slid back in for a few minutes to finish the cooking.

Do not use concrete or standard Portland cement for any assembly of the inner core. Portland cement begins to fail at 700°F (371°C) and your wood-fired brick oven easily can exceed this temperature.

In cold climates, a metal roof is an easy way to protect your oven from moisture damage.

One critical measurement you will want to make is the distance from your elbow to the ground while standing. The finished oven floor should be equal to the height of your bent elbow with your upper arm at your side. This height is just right for placing things in the oven and for seeing into the oven.

The critical part of a wood-fired brick oven is the inner core. The inner core is where the fire and cooking occurs. Inner cores are made with fired clay or firebrick. Our inner core came in sections and was assembled in less than two hours. Sand can be placed around the inner core to increase heat mass and insulated with special materials to hold the heat in. An oven built in this fashion will still be about 300°F (149°C) a day after firing and will remain warm for days from that single firing. Some mornings when I'm barely awake, my wife, Kathy, rushes by me smiling with a tray of cupcake batter on the way to the oven to cook with the heat from the previous day.

Moisture and freezing damages fired-clay products in our cold climate so a roof is essential to keep rain off the inner core. In a dry climate where freezing doesn't occur, no insulation or roof is needed for the oven itself but may be desired as part of the design.

Once the brick oven is built, it basically is free to operate if you have a nearby source of scrap wood. Any kind of dry wood can be used. It will take one to two hours to let it warm up once you have started a fire in it. Most people that come to our house like our homemade thin-crust pizza that is cooked and flame broiled in just four minutes. You can feed a real crowd because you can choose to cook at very high temperatures in this oven.

HOW TO APPROACH BRICK-OVEN BUILDING

1. Check local codes and permitting.
2. Determine location.
3. Determine manufacturer for the inner core.
4. Create design for how you want the finished unit to look.
5. Follow the manufacturer's directions for foundation, support walls and oven sub-floor or make sure your mason does.
6. Finish exterior of oven as desired.

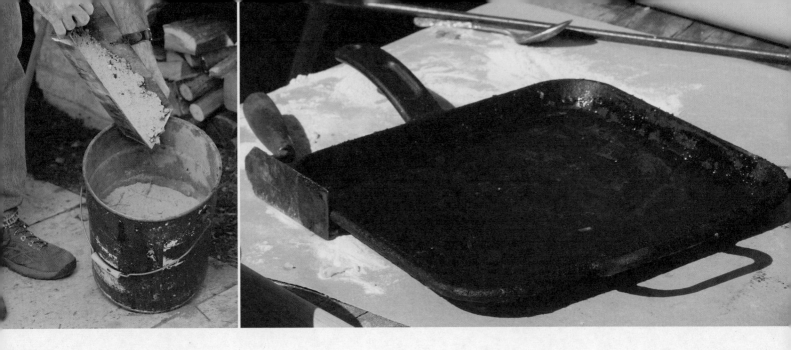

You can install most inner cores yourself and leave the heavy work to your mason, especially if he is not familiar with brick ovens.

ACCESSORIES FOR A WOOD-FIRED BRICK OVEN

1. Ash bucket with tight-fitting lid to hold hot ash.
2. Peel or oven shovel to move things in and out of the oven.
3. Cast-iron cookware for cooking meats and vegetables.
4. Scraper or trowel to clean cast-iron.
5. Standard hoe for scraping the oven floor.
6. Bronze brush with handle for cleaning the oven floor.

You can purchase bronze brushes and peels at your local restaurant supply store. The other items are available through most hardware stores.

Thin-Crust Pizza in the Brick Oven

1. Make or use store-bought dough for crust.
2. Roll out on floured board.
3. Roll out dough to about a ⅛" (3mm) thickness.
4. Add homemade or store-bought spaghetti sauce.
5. Spread the sauce with a spoon.
6. Add pre-cooked sausage if desired.

7. Add cheese.
8. Add mushrooms, raw onion, tomatoes and other vegetables on the very top to flash cook.
9. Flour the peel well or use corn meal on the peel as "ball bearings" so the pizza will slide onto the peel.
10. Put pizza in the oven.
11. Place the peel into the oven and release the pizza with a quick jerking motion. This might take some practice!
12. Keep your eye on the pizza — it will take only about four minutes to cook or five minutes to catch fire!
13. Place the peel in the oven, slide it under the pizza and bring the pizza out of the oven.

For faster results, cook ingredients for the pizza ahead of time in a cast-iron pan in the oven. Here, we show summer squash fries being removed from the oven for an appetizer.

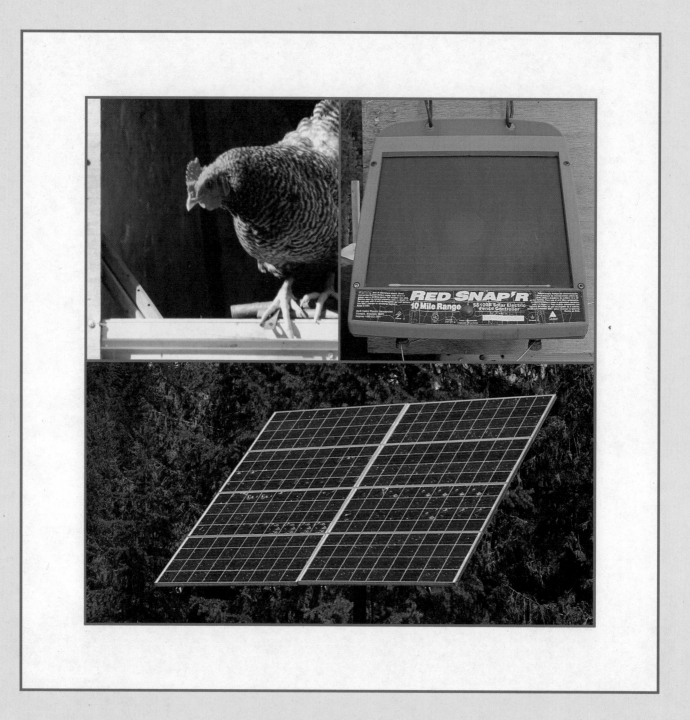

Benefits of Projects for Bold Personalities

SOLAR ELECTRIC FENCE BENEFITS

The solar electric fence has a variety of benefits:
- Low cost compared to running an electrical service.
- Fast and easy to set up; it takes less than an hour.
- These units are sealed against the weather, so they can be left in the rain.
- Can easily be moved to use in another location.

SOLAR PANEL FOR LIGHTING AND PUMPS

Some of the benefits for using a solar panel for lighting and pumps include:
- Easy to hook-up low-voltage wiring.
- You can use any 12-volt accessories, even charge your cell phone!
- Very mobile. Make a cart to take the solar panel, battery and pump where you need it.

LARGE SOLAR PANEL

Here are a few benefits you create with a large solar panel:
- A great way to try large solar panels and the power they can produce.
- Saves on electrical usage and reduces your carbon footprint.
- Can be placed anywhere on your property to produce power where you need it.
- Large panels can be used to store power for emergencies.

Plants for the Bold Personality

If you have a bold personality, you can have plants that exemplify your point of view and project your lifestyle. You will like plants that make a bold statement. Large trees, large shrubs, topiary and large potted plants are all things that show you value living things and you want to show others how to do it. You are not afraid to have large trees or interesting shapes that show what you can do.

LARGE TREES

Large stature trees are in scale with your home and your life's ambitions. Oaks, maples, pines, palms and eucalyptus can be large-sized trees at maturity. These types of trees can be designed into your eco-friendly yard to give it a stately look. If you have a long driveway, you can even line it with large tress. Besides looking impressive, large trees can add tremendous value to your property.

LARGE SHRUBS

Leaving adequate space for large shrubs in your landscape can add to the look you desire. These shrubs come in many varieties and will give your landscape the proper scale. Choosing large shrubs that don't need to be pruned often will reduce maintenance. Pick shrubs that have natural shapes such as vase shaped, globe, small tree form and weeping.

TOPIARY

Topiaries are plants pruned into shapes, usually of animals or geometric patterns. Not everyone has the space, time or money to create and maintain large topiaries. If you do, topiaries can make a very bold statement. There are landscape companies that specialize in selling, creating and maintaining topiaries. If you have the time, you may want to learn to do it yourself.

BOLD PLANTS AND ENERGY CONSERVATION

When you choose large plants for your property, you are also making a statement about energy conservation and your commitment to reducing your carbon footprint. Large trees and shrubs strategically located for your climate can shade your home during the summer, offer windbreaks during the winter and at the same time tie up carbon. These plants can reduce your heating and cooling bill by 25 percent or more. It may be helpful to employ the services of an arborist and landscape designer to plan the design with you.

Remember that symmetric designs, where you have matching topiaries, can be challenging to maintain. If one plant dies in a symmetric design, will you remove the rest and start over, or will you purchase a fully grown plant for replacement?

Chapter 9
The Fun Personality

Whoo! Hoo! Let's celebrate! Do you like to entertain or have a good time no matter what you are doing? Chances are there is a smile on your face right now. If you have a fun personality, you already know it and so will others. Your eco-friendly yard can add to the fun and excitement.

When your family, friends and neighbors are looking for what's happening, they know the party will probably be at your place. Your landscape is a natural extension of your home for entertaining family, friends, neighbors and guests. It's THE fun place to be!

When the office planners want a cookout or somewhere to have a social gathering, yours is the place that could accommodate them. Likewise, if you belong to the soccer or volleyball team. Your place could even include a volleyball court or practice area to add more enjoyment for the team get-together.

The fun part is that you love to come home and enjoy your landscape because it is a wonderful, happy, and fun place to be and it's so easy to add new features for even more fun.

Items you will want to consider for your entertaining landscape include: patio gardens for entertaining, an outdoor shower, outdoor cooking, outdoor lighting, lawn sports areas, and carefree maintenance.

If you are doing the installation or maintenance yourself, finding a fun way to do this will be important for you too.

Create a shower niche by making a path to the shower with privacy fencing.

Standard plumbing fittings can be found at your local hardware store for your shower.

A large flat rock is used for a base to stand on in the shower.

PROJECTS FOR FUN PERSONALITIES
Outdoor Shower

Why Have One?

Does an outdoor shower sound fun to you? We have an outdoor shower in our backyard and it is used daily during the summer. It even includes a foot wash if you just want to wash your feet. We don't have central air conditioning and keeping heat and humidity out of the house is important to keep the house comfortable. Also, I get really dirty at work and so it makes sense not to drag soil and mud all over the house when I get home. It's a great place to cool off after work, exercise or play. Towels stay outside to dry and it's

Gray water is slightly soiled water from showers, laundry and sinks. Ninety percent of the world population does not have drinking water as clean as the gray water that we use once, and then send to the sewage treatment plants in the United States.

This tree uses the gray water from the shower and it has grown at twice the rate of nearby trees because it gets watered daily.

a convenient place to change into or out of swimsuits. Even guests who rush to our house from work so they won't miss the party use the shower. People who live on or near water have remarked that this is a good way to keep all the sand out of their house when the kids and grandkids visit.

You can test how gray water can be utilized in your landscape by watering plants directly from the shower water. You also save money on heating water. If you have a holding tank, you will pump it less if an outdoor shower is used for recycling the used water into your landscape.

If you would like to make your own outdoor shower, take the picture shown to the hardware store and purchase the necessary fittings and pipe. If you don't feel you have enough mechanical abilities for a plumbing project, you can do this the easy way. Create your outdoor shower using a garden hose and other parts you may already have.

SUPPLIES

100 feet (30m) of standard
  garden hose
Watering wand with valve
2 bungee cords
Privacy fencing as desired
Fence posts as needed
Nails and screws
Paving blocks or flat stones
Sand

TOOLS

Posthole digger
Hammer
Drill
Screwdrivers
Shovel

Rubber bungee cords are used for attachment so trees are not harmed.

STEP-BY-STEP INSTRUCTIONS

1. Install privacy fence in desired location.
2. Install a fence post where you want to locate the shower head.
3. Bungee cord the watering wand to the post at a height and location desired for the shower head.
4. Run the garden hose to the watering wand.
5. Leave most of the garden hose in a sunny area so that the water in the hose is solar heated.
6. Attach the garden hose to an outside faucet.
7. Place pavers or flat stones to stand on below the shower head. Use sand to level them.
8. Add a bench, hooks and plants to shower area, if desired.
9. Shovel a drainage area so that the shower water goes to desired plants.
10. Have fun!

Part of a fun landscape can be rustic furniture that you can make yourself from cast off or local materials. Why pay for cheap plastic chairs and tables that only last a couple of years and end up in the landfill? You can make lots of cool furniture that your friends will love. It's easy and it doesn't have to be perfect to be functional. Because you are going to make this furniture with untreated wood products, you can use it as fuel for cooking or heating when the furniture wears out or you don't need it anymore.

SUPPLIES

Wood wire spool in
  desired size
Branches or tree stems
Grapevine or other
  woody vine
Polyurethane glue
2" (50mm) deck, drywall
  or wood screws
¾" (15-20mm) roundhead
  or panhead screws
1½" (40mm) finish
  nails or brads
Tacks
Coat hanger wire
Metal pipe hanger strap

TOOLS

Power saw or handsaw
  for woodworking
Drill
Drill bits slightly smaller in
  diameter than the screws
  and nails for pre-drilling
Wrenches
Hammer
Screwdrivers to fit
  purchased screws
Hacksaw with metal
  cutting blade

Wire Spool Bistro Table

STEP-BY-STEP INSTRUCTIONS

1. Remove the nuts from the iron rods that hold the end of the wire spool.
2. Set aside iron rods for later.
3. Spool will fall apart after removing iron rods — this is a good thing!
4. Remove staves from between the two ends of the wire spool.
5. Cut staves into 6" (15cm) pieces for the table skirt.

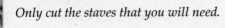

Only cut the staves that you will need.

6. Lay one end of the wire spool with the grooves up on the worktable or floor.
7. Apply polyurethane glue to groove of wire spool end.
8. Take one stave at a time and apply polyurethane glue to one edge and set in the groove.
9. Continue applying glue to one edge and inserting staves until you have completed the circle.

Polyurethane glue is sold under a variety of trade names. It is usually brown or amber in color and has pancake syrup-like consistency and will foam as it hardens. Because moisture is required for a proper bond, this glue will work on damp or wet wood. If an item is very dry that requires gluing, it is necessary to moisten it prior to applying polyurethane glue.

10. To help hold staves, pre-drill with a small drill bit at a 45-degree angle and pound in a finish nail, or drive in a screw to attach each stave to the tabletop.

11. Wrap the table skirt staves with several windings of grapevine and tack in place to secure. (Rope can be used if you don't have vines.)

12. Allow to sit overnight for the glue to harden.

13. Cut branches or tree stems for legs to the height desired for the table. (We used native willow that arches to make bowed legs.)

14. Attach the legs by drilling holes through the staves and installing screws through the staves and into the legs.

15. Use a metal pipe hanger strap on the inside and install with screws for extra support.

16. Drill holes the diameter of the iron rod that held the spool together about ½" (13mm) deep on the inside of the legs about 12" (31cm) above the floor.
17. Cut iron rods to length and lightly spread the table legs and insert the rods.
18. Tie rods where they cross with a bit of coat hanger wire.
19. Wrap vines or rope around the legs in this area to hold rods and legs in place. Tack in place.
20. Stand table upright, and trim the legs with the saw so the table doesn't wobble.
21. Apply stain and varnish, if desired.
22. The hole in the center of table can hold a candle or an umbrella.

SUPPLIES

Branches or tree stems
Piece of thick board 1½" (35-
    40mm) thick, 12" (30cm)
    long and 10" (25cm) wide
2 pieces of thin board
    ¾" (15-20mm) thick,
    10" (25cm) long, and
    1½" (35-40mm) wide
Polyurethane glue
Deck, drywall or wood
    screws or finish nails 1½"
    to 2" long (35-50mm)
Antique cast-iron farm
    implement seat (from
    farm sales, auctions
    or the Internet)

TOOLS

Tenon-making tool
Saw
Drill
Spade bit sized to make the
    hole (called mortise) for
    the tenon. Use the size and
    kind of bit recommended
    by the manufacturer of
    the tenon-making tool
Screwdriver for the type of
    screw heads that you use
Hammer

Bistro Chairs

Make chairs to match your new bistro table.

STEP-BY-STEP INSTRUCTIONS

1. Cut a 12" x 10" (30cm x 25cm) section of thick board.
2. Drill a hole in each corner at a slight outward angle to fit the tenon.
   You may want to try this on a scrap piece first by making the leg in
   step 5 to see if your angle will be right for how you want the chair
   to turn out.

3. Glue and nail two thin boards to the bottom of the thick board and perpendicular to the grain of the thick board for extra strength. Do not cover the holes you drilled in step 2.

4. Cut branches or tree stems to the length desired for the chair legs.

5. Using the tenon-making tool, create the tenon on one end of each leg.

6. Place leg tenons into each hole of the thick board.

7. Measure the distance between each leg, about 12" (30cm) above the feet, and add approximately 1½" (5cm) to each measurement. This will account for the space the tenon takes up.

8. Cut four crosspieces for the chair legs based on measurements of installed legs in step 6.

9. Using the tenon-making tool, create the tenon for each end of the crosspieces.

10. Drill holes at 90 degrees on each leg about 12" (30cm) off the floor.

11. Stagger holes so that the front and back are the same and the sides are about 1" (3cm) higher.

12. Lightly spread the chair legs to install the crosspiece tenons into the holes drilled in the legs. Place a little glue in each hole that a tenon will go into. Tap legs or crosspieces into place.

13. Pre-drill holes for screws or nails so they pass through the tenon and leg. Install screws or nails. You can put the nails and screws in at an angle, perpendicular to the tenon or from the opposite side of the leg from where the tenon enters. Make sure the screw tip does not protrude from the leg.

14. Screw or nail tenons on the legs to the thick board in the same fashion as step 13.

15. Stand chair upright and trim legs so the chair doesn't wobble.

16. Screw implement seat to the top of the thick board.

17. See Cork End Table project for more details regarding tenon tool and assembly.

SUPPLIES

Branches or tree stems

Corks (Don't drink wine? Find a person
or business that serves wine and
ask them to save you some corks.)

Expanded metal lathe for desired
table size (from the hardware
store or concrete supplier)

Small pieces of wood trim about
the thickness of corks, ¾" (20mm)
and enough for the perimeter
of the table times two

Nails and screws are optional for
legs and crosspieces (Can be
the same ones used in making
the bistro chair project)

Construction adhesive or hot glue sticks

1½" (40mm) finish nails

¼" to ⅜" (6-9mm) staples
for staple gun

Sheet of plywood or stiff cardboard
for desired size table

Polyurethane glue

TOOLS

Power saw or handsaw
for woodworking

Hammer

Staple gun and staples

Tin snips

Caulk gun or hot glue gun

Drill

Tenon-cutting tool

Vise

Cork End Table

End tables can have any type of top including a flat piece of stone.

STEP-BY-STEP INSTRUCTIONS

1. Cut four larger diameter tree stems to length for the table legs.
2. Cut eight smaller stems for crosspieces to lengths desired.

Tenon-cutting tool and tenon or dowel created with the tool.

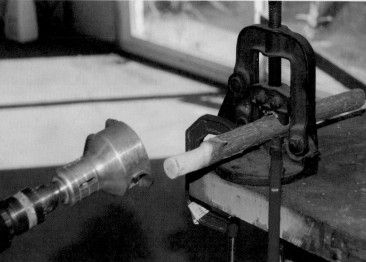

Use a pipe clamp or vise to hold the stem being cut.

Slowly feed tenon tool into stem.

Make different lengths of tenons by increasing
or decreasing how far you cut into the stem.

A heavy-duty drill or a smaller drill with a ½" (13mm) chuck can be used if you don't mind taking more time.

Drill holes (mortise) in legs using a spade bit the same size as the tenon.

Space and drill two pairs of holes 90 degrees to each other in each leg.

Polyurethane glue can be used on wet or damp wood.

3. Use tenon-cutting tool and vise to cut tenons on both ends of crosspieces.

4. Drill holes for crosspieces in desired locations.

5. Apply polyurethane glue to holes.

Insert crosspiece and tap into place.

You can make one side at a time placing the crosspieces in first and then fitting the corresponding leg.

When making rustic furniture, it doesn't have to be perfect. However, you can turn crosspieces while assembling or weight down the piece before the glue dries to help take out the twist caused by irregular pieces of wood. This way, all of the legs will meet the floor.

6. Install crosspieces to one side of the table at a time.
7. Use hammer, as necessary, to tap crosspieces into place.
8. Place table base on flat surface and place weights on it while the glue dries.
9. Make two identical frames for the tabletop that are just a little wider and longer than the table.
10. Cut and nail wood trim for the tabletop frames.
11. Using tin snips, cut a piece of the expanded metal lathe the size of the frame.
12. Staple the lathe to one frame.
13. Place the other frame over the top to sandwich the metal lathe between the two frames.

Trim metal lathe so sharp edges don't protrude beyond the frame.

For larger tabletops, add additional bracing underneath.

Gluing the corks looks messy, but it's fast and no one will see it.

14. Nail the two frames together.
15. Place corks in the pattern that you desire on top of the tray formed by the lathe and wood frame.
16. Leave corks loose — don't force them.
17. Place a stiff sheet of cardboard or plywood over the top of the corks.
18. Holding the cardboard or plywood in place, turn the table over onto a worktable.
19. You will be able to see the back of the corks through the metal lathe.
20. Using construction adhesive or hot glue, force the adhesive through the lathe to secure the corks to the lathe.
21. Allow to dry.
22. Turn over and take off cardboard or plywood.
23. Your tabletop is ready to go on the table stand.
24. Oops! Did you make the tabletop too small for the table like I did? Just cut grooves or notches in the top of the legs to fit the tabletop.

Benefits of Projects for Fun Personalities

OUTDOOR SHOWER

An outdoor shower can create benefits for you and your visitors:
- Inexpensive to build.
- Low maintenance and easy to use.
- More refreshing than an indoor shower on a hot day.
- Can be decorated with fun things or living plants.
- Less indoor cleaning and musty towels to deal with.
- Water runoff is diverted to neighboring plants.

RUSTIC FURNITURE PROJECT

Rustic furniture doesn't have to be perfect, so have fun building it.
- Low cost to build.
- Get your materials right from your own yard or the neighbor's.
- Can be left out in the weather to create an even more natural appearance.
- Rustic furniture is a popular choice to reuse and recycle products.
- Customize to fit your style or hobbies.

Plants for the Fun Personality

You like to have fun with what you do, so choose fun plants that you and your friends will enjoy. You may want to choose plants that bloom at different times for full-season color, plants with unique bark, leaves or stems and fruits and vegetables that have fun colors.

FLOWERING PLANTS

Whatever climate you live in, there are all sorts of perennials, shrubs, trees and bulbs that produce flowers. You can get help designing the right mix so that everyday there is a display of color in your yard. Many flowering plants will have colorful fruit after the flowers fade, adding joy for you and the wildlife.

WINTER COLOR

Winter does not have to be dreary either. You can mix in plants that have colorful bark, over-wintering fruit or whimsical shapes that are best seen during the winter. Our red-stem dogwoods in our yard provide a stunning display of red and pink stems during the winter months and are especially showy against an evergreen background.

FRUIT AND VEGETABLES

Perennial fruits and vegetables only need to be planted once and then the fun begins. There is purple asparagus, many fruit varieties (even kiwis), colorful apples and tasty berries. Your yard can be a riot of fruit and vegetable color as you amble through the vegetation and graze as you go. What fun!

FUN PLANTS AND ENERGY CONSERVATION

Can you imagine not having to drive across town to the florist to decorate the inside of your home? Not only that, but if you pick your own flowers you know they came from your yard and not thousands of miles away where they were treated with nasty pesticides. Shrub and tree blossoms also can be easily cut to enjoy indoors. You may even try your hand at "forcing" blossoms by bringing cuttings indoors during the winter months. Making your own flowering bouquets, dried arrangements and picking your own fruit can have a huge impact by reducing the amount of energy you use to obtain these things as well as the energy used for shipping to your local market. You can have fun and be sustainable at the same time! Your fruit-producing plants are also natural bird feeders and you can feel good about that. You probably love birds, and when you choose to grow your own bird food, birds won't be killed or displaced by the growing of commercial bird seed.

Chapter 10
The Perfectionist Personality

I used to think that people who wanted perfect and manicured landscapes were just, well, too perfect. But think about it, doesn't everyone have things that they want that are just right? Have you ever watched a bird build a nest? They work away until it is just right. Their instincts tell them that to raise their young, the nest needs to be built perfectly.

There are no alternatives when it comes to your landscape. It has to be perfect for you, and in your eyes, ideal for everyone else too! Every aspect must look and feel right for you to be comfortable, even if it means pulling weeds on a Sunday morning or mowing the grass one more time each week.

Your eco-friendly yard easily can accommodate the perfect nature that you may have and it can also be the perfect complement to your lifestyle. You may choose plant species that have just the right size and form that you desire instead of trying to continually prune a plant that doesn't fit. Your sustainable landscape also can provide nutrients and precise watering of your plants. All of this and you can be good to the environment too.

The challenge for people who want a manicured landscape is: will they be patient enough to let natural methods work? Many times we seek the quick way of doing things that causes more problems in the long-term. For instance, corn gluten works great as a pre-emergent for crabgrass. However, it is not as effective the first year of use as chemical alternatives. Corn gluten works slower, but also provides nitrogen and organic material to enrich soils. After several years, corn gluten is as effective as harsh and toxic pesticides and it will provide a safer and better lawn. Another example is the use of synthetic weed barriers and stone mulch for landscape beds. Initially, this approach looks great, but after a few years, the stone gets filled with organic material and gets weedy, the plants don't thrive because they are suffocated by plastic, and the landscape declines so much that it needs to be replaced in five years. Is this your idea of perfect?

Sustainable landscape principles can be applied to help you achieve the perfect landscape for your lifestyle. It just takes a little more effort to realize all of the benefits and have the landscape that is just right for you.

Drip irrigation in our nursery directly waters the plants and reduces weeds.

A very thin line and weighted emitter provide about one quart (1L) of water to each plant every day.

PROJECTS FOR PERFECTIONIST PERSONALITIES
Drip Irrigation

Drip irrigation is a great way to precisely control water application to plants. Although drip irrigation is not a new idea in water-deprived areas of the world, it does have new applications even in water-rich areas. Drip irrigation is the method of applying a small amount of water directly to the root system of plants. There is very little waste and evaporation and it's very environmentally friendly. Instead of spraying water all over the yard, you target your water application. You save water and money and it makes your plants healthier. Many plants are damaged or are more susceptible to disease by overhead watering. Mildew and slug damage to plants are often the most visible signs of a too-moist climate because of overhead watering. Drip irrigation can be regulated to provide just the right amount of water for any type of soil, climate or plant.

Drip irrigation uses less water than sprinkler systems but does need to be monitored. When using drip irrigation, it is a good idea to check your drip system once a week for leaks, damage, or plugged emitters.

SUPPLIES

Drip irrigation line
Pressure-compensating emitters,
   1 gallon (4L) per hour
Pressure regulator with
   garden hose threads,
   per manufacturer's
   recommendation
Female hose end
Male hose end
End cap
Landscape staples
Couplers

TOOLS

Drip irrigation punch
Pruning shears
Hammer

Shown, from left, end cap fitting, drip irrigation line, female garden hose fitting, pressure regulator, and garden hose.

Cut tape on irrigation line when you are ready to unroll it and follow step 4 so it does not tangle and kink.

STEP-BY-STEP INSTRUCTIONS

1. Apply female garden hose end to outer end of drip irrigation coil.
2. Install pressure regulator to your outdoor faucet or garden hose.
3. Thread female garden hose end of drip irrigation coil to the pressure regulator.
4. Carefully roll out drip irrigation coil like you would roll a spare tire for a car.
5. Install landscape staples to hold the drip irrigation line as you go.
6. Place the line as close as possible to the plants you want to water.
7. When you have placed the irrigation line by all of the plants, cut off the extra line with a pruning shears.
8. Install an end cap fitting to the cut end.
9. Go back to the start of your drip irrigation line.
10. Using the punch tool, punch a hole in the drip line near the plant you want to water.

Drip irrigation uses a pre-set pressure regulator to reduce water pressure so that hose clamps are usually not needed to hold fittings to the line.

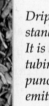

Drip irrigation line is not standard irrigation hose. It is a special thin-wall tubing that allows you to punch holes and install emitters without leaking.

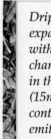

Drip irrigation line expands and contracts with temperature changes. Place a curve in the line every 50 feet (15m) for expansion or contraction so that the emitters are not pulled away from their location.

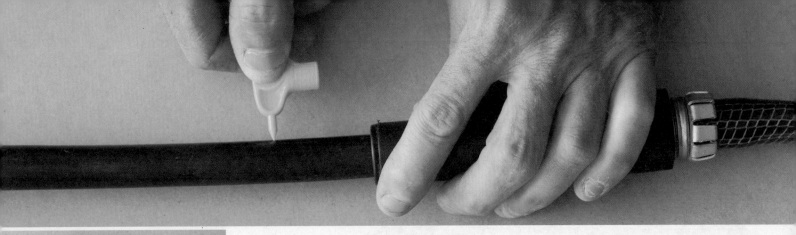

A simple punch tool designed for drip irrigation.

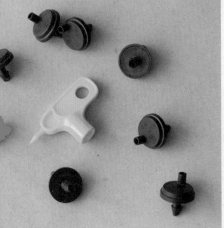

Close-up of pressure-compensating emitters and punch tool.

You can hear a "snap" when the emitter is properly installed.

11. Place an emitter with the barbed end first into the punched hole until it snaps into position.
12. Repeat steps 10 and 11 until all of the plants have an emitter.
13. With the end cap off, turn on the water and flush any debris from the drip irrigation line.
14. Replace the end cap and check that each emitter is working properly.
15. If an emitter is damaged, cut it off with a pruning shears leaving the barbed end in the irrigation line. Be careful not to damage the irrigation line. Snap a new one in place in the same hole. The cut off barbed part can be flushed out by removing the end cap and turning on the water.

To ensure the best installation, use pressure-compensating emitters so that the amount of water coming out of the first emitter on the line is the same as the amount of water coming out of the last emitter on the line. Fancy emitters that are adjustable are not needed and are more likely to plug up and create problems for you.

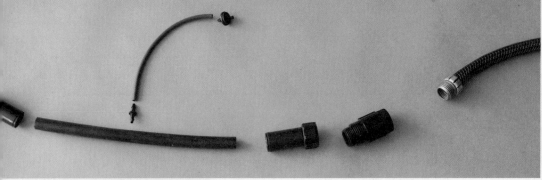
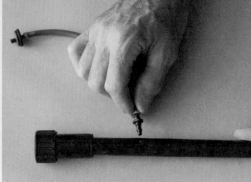

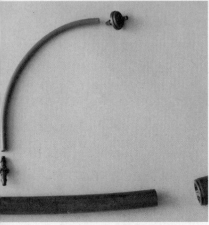

Two-way barbed fitting, small diameter drip tube and emitters are all that is needed to give just the right amount of water to your planters.

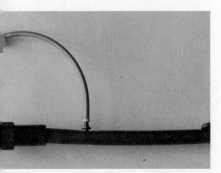

Complete installation.

Drip irrigation for planters and window boxes.

If desired, pre-assemble and then attach to your drip irrigation system.

Drip Irrigation for Planters

Planters or window boxes are ideal for using drip irrigation that provides just the right amount of water.

STEP-BY-STEP INSTRUCTIONS

1. Install drip irrigation system as instructed in Drip Irrigation Project.
2. Place standard drip irrigation line as needed.
3. Use punch tool to make hole in drip irrigation line.
4. Snap in barbed fitting.
5. Wiggle on one end of small diameter drip line to opposite end of barbed fitting which is also barbed.
6. Extend small diameter drip line to planter or window box.
7. Drill hole for entry through deck or near top of planter.
8. Place a ½ gallon (2L) per hour emitter into the small diameter drip line, barbed end first.
9. Secure with landscape staples.

SUPPLIES

Drip irrigation system as previously described on page 130
Small diameter drip line
Barbed fittings for small diameter drip line
Pressure-compensating drip emitters, ½ gallon (2L) per hour
Landscape staples

TOOLS

Pruning shears
Drill and drill bits

DETERMINING AMPLE WATER SUPPLY FOR DRIP IRRIGATION

If you have a well, contact your well-driller or find the original report for the construction of your well. Some municipalities will have this report on file. Your entire household can not remove more water from your well than the recharge capacity of the well which is rated in gallons per minute (gpm). Running your well dry can damage the well itself as well as the pump.

If you have municipal water, you can measure the amount of water that comes out of your garden faucet in 15 seconds. Multiply that volume of water by four, and you will know the gallons per minute (gpm) that your faucet can provide.

Example: One gallon (4L) produced in 15 seconds equals four gallons (15L) per minute (gpm) or 240 gallons (908L) per hour (gph).

If you are using one gallon (4L) gph drip emitters, the maximum that you could run at one time would be 240 emitters, if you used the example above.

If you are using the Mizzle Wizard micro-irrigation sprinklers that use one gallon (4L) gpm, then each one will use 60 (227L) gph and you could only run four at a time using the above example.

If you have a cistern for your water supply, you can use some of the same calculations from the above and then figure in how much water is available between rainfalls for your irrigation system.

Water from municipal systems in the United States often contains small amounts of added chlorine and other chemicals. Plants and people were not designed to ingest chlorine, and there may be many medical side effects of consuming chlorine. We have noticed some plants on certain soils do not thrive and have more health issues when fed a regular diet of chlorinated water. While it is practical for you to remove chlorine from your drinking water at home, it is difficult to treat the amount of water that you might use for irrigation. Roof water stored in cisterns and ponds is a better choice, if you have space. A second choice is to run chlorinated water into an open tank or pond to let the chlorine evaporate. Gravity, or a pump, can then be used to transport the water to your irrigation system.

HOW LONG AND HOW OFTEN SHOULD I RUN MY IRRIGATION SYSTEM?

You should run your drip or micro-irrigation system just long enough to maintain an adequate level of moisture in your soil for optimal plant growth based on your goals. If your goal is to produce a volume of produce from a few plants, careful and adequate watering will help provide you with a better crop. If you are only intent on your plants surviving until it rains, then you can use a little supplemental watering. Heavy and clay soils need to be monitored more carefully for over watering than sandy, well-drained soils. Over watering on heavy soils can result in the same root rots that you see in potted house plants that your black-thumbed neighbor over watered for you while you were on vacation.

The best advice is to monitor the moisture of your plants on your site. Stick a shovel into the soil next to a plant that is being irrigated. How does the soil look a few inches down? Is it dusty and dry indicating that more watering is needed, or did the hole fill with water and visions of your black-thumbed neighbor came to mind? Wilting plants can indicate over-watered or under-watered plants. Dry soil conditions in irrigated areas can mean that the sprinkler is not reaching the plant or that a drip emitter is plugged. If other plants on the same system are adequately watered and some are not, you'll want to do some investigating to see what is going on.

Irrigation, no matter how efficient, is not a substitute for poor decision making or poor soil practices. Drip and micro-irrigation are intended to help prevent mortality in established plants and help them survive during a drought. Mulching soils and installing suitable plants for your environment is the best thing that you can do to reduce the cost and environmental issues of irrigation.

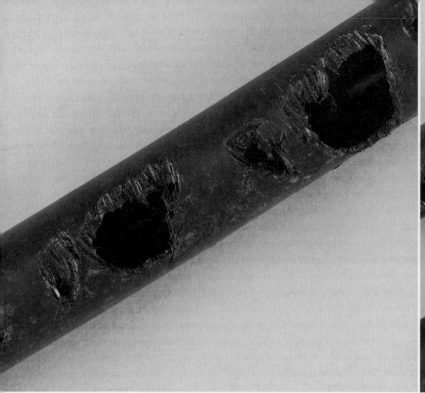

Squirrel damage to a drip line.

Maintenance for Drip and Micro-Irrigation Systems

Drip and micro-irrigation use substantially less water, but the trade-off is that these systems should be checked regularly to ensure a high level of efficiency. Minor repairs may be necessary and are very easy for you to do.

Squirrels regularly chew through wires in transformers frying themselves in the process. Why wouldn't they chew through some nice safe drip irrigation? You can bury irrigation lines where rabbits, squirrels and rodents are present to avoid most damage. And no, it doesn't seem to help by leaving drinking water out for these juvenile delinquents of the animal world. Rodents aren't looking for water in irrigation lines any more than they are looking to charge up their cell phones by gnawing into electrical lines.

SUPPLIES

Drip irrigation line
Pressure-compensating emitters,
   1 gallon (4L) per hour
Pressure regulator with
   garden hose threads, per
   manufacturer's recommendation
Female hose end
Male hose end
End cap
Landscape staples
Couplers

TOOLS

Drip irrigation punch
Pruning shears
Hammer

STEP-BY-STEP INSTRUCTIONS

1. Check for leaks and cut off damaged pipe sections or fitting with a pruning shears.

2. Replace fitting, or add a section of new pipe and attach with couplings.

3. Clogged sprinklers can be removed and cleaned. Plugged emitters can be cut off and replaced.

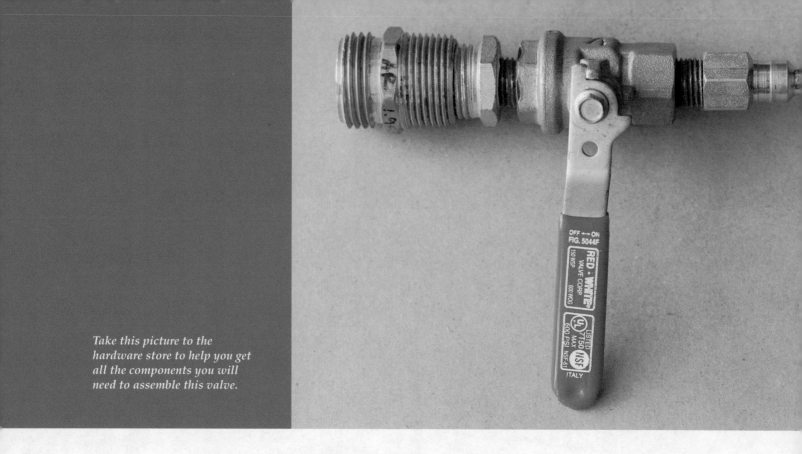

Take this picture to the hardware store to help you get all the components you will need to assemble this valve.

SUPPLIES

None

TOOLS

Small air compressor (Don't buy one — use your neighbor's! Everyone seems to have one these days.)

Valve with compressor fitting on one end and male hose end on the other

Safety glasses

Earplugs

"Blowing Out" Irrigation Lines

In climates where soil temperatures get below freezing, damage to irrigation lines can be significantly reduced by removing most of the water prior to freezing.

If you already have an irrigation company that winterizes your system, they can also take care of your drip and micro-irrigation while they are at your home. Large irrigation systems require compressors with lots of air volume to force water from the lines. If you have a small drip or micro-irrigation system like we have discussed in this book, you can "blow it out" yourself with minimal equipment.

Parts for a valve like the one shown to blow out your drip or micro-irrigation can be purchased at your local hardware store.

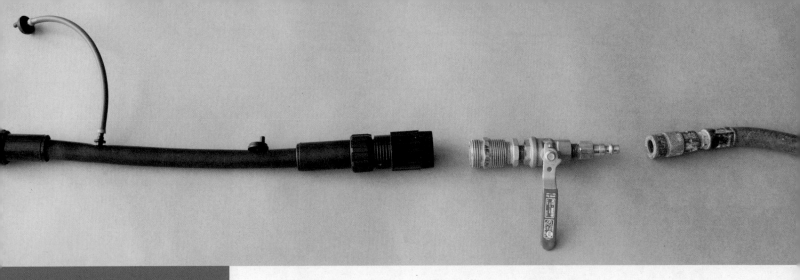

STEP-BY-STEP INSTRUCTIONS

1. Put on your safety glasses and earplugs.
2. Remove end caps from your drip or micro-irrigation system.
3. Thread male hose end of valve into female hose end of irrigation system located near your faucet where you started the system.
4. Couple compressor fitting of valve to hose on compressor.
5. Set compressor at 40 psi (276kPa) so you don't damage your irrigation system.
6. Turn on compressor and allow tank to fill.
7. Open the valve, allowing air from the compressor to rush through the irrigation line and force water out.
8. Close the valve and allow pressure to build in compressor tank again.
9. Open valve and allow air to blow through the irrigation line again.
10. Repeat steps 8 and 9 until no water or mist is coming out of end-cap fitting.
11. Turn off compressor.
12. Relieve pressure at the compressor.
13. Remove valve.
14. Replace end cap.
15. Cover female garden hose end near the faucet with tape or a plastic bag to keep debris out for the winter.
16. In spring, your system will be ready to reattach to the water supply and be usable.

You can build this sturdy tool holder faster than you can drive to the store and buy one and it will be just right!

Well-Organized Tool Storage

You like things well organized. Your home is neat and everything is in its place. Your landscape reflects this too. Are you having trouble organizing your yard tools? You can create sturdy tool holders from tree and shrub stems right from your own yard. These tool holders can be placed in your shop, garage or potting shed. These natural-looking tool holders can even be placed outside so that your tools are organized and ready to use when you need them. By making your own tool holders from yard leftovers, you significantly cut down on cost, transportation, fuel costs and imported materials. The best part is that you can make these tool holders exactly the way you want them.

This tenon-cutting tool makes a tenon to exactly fit a one-inch (25mm) diameter hole.

STEP-BY-STEP INSTRUCTIONS

1. Check out instructions for using the tenon-cutting tool in Chapter 9 under Cork End Table Project.
2. Cut tree or shrub stems to length for use as tool holder pegs.
3. Use tenon cutter to create tenons on tool holder pegs.
4. Drill corresponding holes in a board, timber or larger branch to use as a backboard.
5. Apply polyurethane glue to holes and tap in tool holder pegs.
6. Install a nail or screw at a 45-degree angle to the tenon to secure the tool-holder peg to the backboard.

SUPPLIES

Tree or shrub stems
Board, timber or larger branch
Polyurethane glue
Screws or nails

TOOLS

Drill
Spade bits
Tenon-cutting tool
Screwdrivers
Hammer

My trailer is set up as a mobile tool shed.

SUPPLIES

Tool holders as described
   earlier in this chapter,
   or conventional hooks
Paint and painting supplies
Notecards
Stapler and staples
Drywall, plywood
   or chipboard
Nails or screws sized for the
   thickness of the drywall,
   plywood or chipboard
   you are using and the
   weight it will hold. (You
   can get advice from the
   lumber yard regarding
   your specific situation.)

TOOLS

Drill
Spade bits
Tenon-cutting tool
Screwdrivers for
   screws purchased
Hammer
Pencil or marker

Master Tool Storage

An efficient landscape is a sustainable one. Every minute you spend
finding or digging out a tool is a minute that you will never get back
and a minute wasted on not accomplishing your goals in your yard.
Part of tool use is having the right tool for the job and being able to
find it fast. Otherwise, you spend valuable time looking for things
rather than working on your eco-friendly yard.

Painted shadows for the tools make it easier to put them back in the right place.

You are probably particular where your tools end up after use, particularly when there are other people using them. Create an easy way to find out if your tools made it back where they belong. Some years ago, when I had up to seven employees, I found it necessary to get our work trailer very organized so that all of the tools made it home at the end of the day and that we had the right tools to take to the job. This system of tool storage has now been in use for years and even for me it is extremely helpful. I know immediately where a tool goes, if it is missing, and even the name of the tool if I am training someone new. You won't find any tool boxes in my work trailer because tool boxes become a dumping ground for all sorts of stuff, and there is no way to know if things are missing until you are miles from anywhere.

I use bungee cords attached to conduit straps to hold the tools in place while going down the road.

Paint shadows for small tools and use short sections of discarded PVC pipe to hold the tools.

STEP-BY-STEP INSTRUCTIONS

1. Install drywall, plywood or chipboard on the wall where tools will be hung.

2. Create tool holders as needed.

3. Hang tools in an arrangement most convenient for you.

4. Use a pencil or marker to outline each tool.

5. Remove the tools and paint on the outline.

6. Staple notecards with the tool's name by each outline.

7. Re-hang the tools.

Benefits of Projects for Perfectionist Personalities

DRIP IRRIGATION

Drip irrigation creates benefits that are just right for you:
- The right amount of water where you need it.
- No waste.
- Drip irrigation can be set up in about the time that it takes to hand-water once.
- Can be added to those hard-to-water pots, planters and hanging baskets so they look great all the time.

WELL-ORGANIZED TOOL STORAGE

Well-organized tool storage benefits:
- Creates an attractive way to store your tools.
- Uses materials from your yard.
- Saves time by having tools exactly where you need them most often.

MASTER TOOL STORAGE

Master tool storage has benefits to you and other users of your tools:
- All of the tools go back exactly in the right place.
- You know immediately if a tool is missing.
- Helps others when you ask them to retrieve a tool by a certain name.
- You easily can inspect your tools for repair or service.

Plants for the Perfectionist Personality

Plants that you enjoy look perfect all of the time, even if it means that they receive some extra care from you to look that way. It is really important that you make your plant selections carefully to get the kinds of plants you want.

DWARF TREES AND SHRUBS

You will find that dwarf trees and shrubs are a smart choice for you, especially if you have limited space. Look for plants that are labeled dwarf or compact. Generally, these plants have natural characteristics that result in a slow, tight growth pattern. There are many shapes available, so make your selection based on how you want the mature plant to look. Plants like this can look good without pruning and can be spaced in a way that provides you with the perfect setting. Many of these dwarf trees and shrubs also can be grown in clean-lined planters to give a more finished look to the perfect landscape.

SMALL PERENNIALS

Plant small perennials that form a tight grouping, or plant grass types that form a clump to create a carefully orchestrated landscape. Perennials may need occasional deadheading to remove spent flowers, but by making careful choices, you will have the right plant in the right place.

HEDGES

Choose the proper plants to create neat-looking hedges. Some shrubs grow very rapidly and are difficult to maintain as a pruned hedge. Shrubs, like boxwood (Buxus sp.) are quite common over a large geographic range and have been used for hundreds of years as a neatly pruned hedge. Choose hedge plants carefully so you don't have to work too hard at keeping it perfectly shaped.

PERFECT PLANTS FOR ENERGY CONSERVATION

Dwarf and compact plants can be big energy savers. Some dwarf plants can be used to shade patios, windows and the walls of your home which will save on cooling costs. Plants that require little or no pruning or other care take less energy to maintain. Plants that don't grow out of control and then have to be cut down and disposed of can save you more energy. When you do have to prune these plants, snip off little pieces at a time using the chop-and-drop method, and let the pieces fall where no one will see them. By using these plants for self-mulching, you save yourself and the environment the costs of mulch.

Chapter 11
The Easy-Going Personality

About 60 percent of people exhibit a peaceful easy-going personality. They go to work, take care of their children and other obligations, avoid seeking confrontation except when needed and want to come home, relax and avoid hassles.

Does this describe your personality? You work hard every day, which is why your home and landscape is a peaceful retreat. When you get home, you just want to relax, cast aside the worries of the day and swing in your hammock. Your landscape totally complements your lifestyle. It does not require much maintenance, it is hassle free, and it enables you to take it easy and enjoy life.

If you have an easy-going peaceful personality, you will want your landscape to be respectable, and above all, a smart choice. You'll probably want quiet areas to relax and enjoy a warm summer evening, kindle a fire, or listen to the birds. You'll also want a yard that pretty much takes care of itself. You can kick back, friends will love to come over and relax with a cold beverage — or a hot one — and there are no frustrations!

Things you may want to consider for your serene landscape include: orderly patio gardens, hedges and fences for screening and privacy, areas to enhance wildlife viewing, water gardens and features, drip irrigation, regimented and reduced lawn areas, native and natural plantings, well-behaved perennials, weed control, and outdoor fireplaces and fire pits.

Challenge areas for an easy-going personality are creating a landscape that is low maintenance so that it does not become a problem, has ease of maintenance, and where maintenance can be done when it fits your schedule. If your landscape is difficult to build, hard to maintain, or gives you bad feelings when you see it, this will not fit your personality. Your landscape is your retreat destination and you don't want to dread going there.

Soils with added organic mater will have more earthworms, which in turn enrich the soil even more.

Our chickens and local crows become slightly intoxicated eating the fermented berries that weren't sorted from the leaves.

PROJECTS FOR EASY-GOING PERSONALITIES

TYPES OF MULCH

Mulch for a sustainable landscape is any material that will naturally decompose and help hold moisture, reduce erosion, smother weeds, and nourish your soil. You can't have enough organic material on your property to use as mulches. You can save money and create all sorts of functional benefits if you don't throw away or burn mulch materials, or let the city haul it off. You just need to know what kinds of low-cost organic materials are available where you live.

Twigs, branches, grass clippings, leaves, corn stalks, cattails, untreated lumber, newspapers, magazines, paper towels, deer hides, your old blue jeans or cotton shirts, bark, sawdust, pine needles, dead weeds, cardboard, wool or jute rugs, Zebra Mussel shells, feathers, hair, shredded office paper, junk mail, old books, catalogs, straw, citrus peels, nut shells and hay are all mulching material. In many suburban areas, there is plenty of free mulch during fall and spring clean-up days. You don't have to drive far to get it, and you may even get people to bring the mulch to you.

Cranberry bogs near our home have cranberry leaves as a by-product of harvest and it makes a good mulch. Cranberry leaves have a thick waxy cuticle (leaf covering) that slows decomposition. We have piles of leaves in storage at our place.

Zebra Mussels are an introduced species to fresh water in North America. They are an invasive species and viewed as troublesome by some people. Many people rake the shells up from their beach so people won't cut their feet. I think as long as we can't get rid of them — let's use them to our benefit.

Compost in bins can be difficult to move around or turn.

COMPOSTING OR DECOMPOSITION

Composting is the process of placing the proper types of mulch together to create bacterial action. A side effect of bacterial action is the production of heat. Bacterial action and heat will help with rapid decomposition of mulch materials and may or may not kill diseases and weed seeds. If you feel a compost pile is too much work, my suggestion is to use the compost material as mulch. Place it where you want it and let it naturally decompose. This is a great way to start raised beds. Nature doesn't compost; it decomposes. As an example, take branches and place them on the ground and layer other organic material over the branches to hasten the decomposition.

Bacterial action and fungal action are natural decomposition methods. Bacterial action is most commonly found in grass clippings and garden waste. Fungal action is usually found in woody material and tree and shrub leaves, which is why leaf mold refers to fungal action on decomposed leaves.

Some plants easily die under clear plastic; others thrive!

Black plastic kills off weed tops, but not roots or seeds.

In areas with low amounts of rainfall, clear or black plastic can be used to create condensation and keep mulch materials moist, aiding in decomposition.

WEED CONTROL PRIOR TO MULCHING

By doing some simple things, you can significantly reduce weeds in mulched areas. It is not necessary to remove weeds or grasses before mulching as long as you combine other methods that work to discourage weed growth through the mulch you are using. Plants can grow through mulches because of strong growth characteristics exhibited by trees, shrubs and many perennials. Weeds also come up from under mulches because the proper conditions have been met for growth. Porous mulches allow sunlight through, stimulating seed germination. A nice aspect of using organic mulches is that it's easy to fix the problem of weeds.

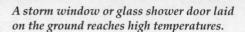

A storm window or glass shower door laid on the ground reaches high temperatures.

Weed tops are completely gone, but what about the roots?

This method would work well for weedy areas in existing mulch.

THE BLACK PLASTIC MYTH FOR REDUCING WEEDS

Some people wrongly suggest using black plastic temporarily to solarize (using the sun's heat) to kill weed seeds in the garden or yard. This is just another gardening "old wives tale." Tests on our property show that the soil under black plastic is actually cooler than bare soil that has no covering. On an 80°F (27°C) day, bare soil at ½" (13mm) below the surface was 120°F (49°C) in full sun. Under the black plastic, the soil was 98°F (37°C) at the same depth. The black plastic actually shaded the soil and made it cooler. The average person cannot heat up the soil enough to make a difference using this limited solar method. Some plant seeds are even stimulated by high temperatures and we see this effect in grass and forest fires. Air temperatures under clear plastic get hotter than black plastic and will damage the above-soil growth of some plants. However, others may thrive in the tropical climate created. We achieved the best result with a storm window. Weed tops were scorched in a day or two, but new sprouts kept appearing for several weeks. You can use black plastic to deprive plants of light and eventually kill them, but this may take days or weeks depending on the variety of plants.

AVOID SYNTHETIC WEED BARRIERS

Synthetic weed barriers are sold to prevent weeds in your garden, and all they do is increase the cost and maintenance of your landscape. You can avoid all of the problems associated with synthetic, woven weed barriers by simply not using them. Synthetic weed barriers prevent normal biological actions to occur between organic mulches or composts and the soil. Roots of desirable plants often grow over the top of synthetic weed barriers and roots of trees under the barrier are often very shallow. This can result in damage or loss of the plant. Synthetic weed barriers restrict the necessary spreading nature of many perennials resulting in a significantly shorter life span. To top it off, many

Kill weeds in mulched beds by smothering them with newspaper or sheets of cardboard. Then, sprinkle a little more mulch over the top to hide the paper.

weeds readily seed and grow over the top of synthetic weed barriers, and it is difficult to remove them as their roots intertwine with the barrier. The silliness of purchasing and using synthetic weed barriers is only exceeded by buying a larger riding mower so you can cut even more grass.

EASY MULCHING AND COMPOSTING

Leave It Where You Found It!

The fastest way to reduce the time and effort you are now spending on your landscape is to handle mulching and composting differently. There is no shortage of people and methods that tell you how to compost, all of the steps involved, and what kind of expensive bins to buy. Mulching and composting don't have to be complicated and time-consuming projects. At my work sites, I leave sod, organic materials, and even root systems in place. All of these things provide natural fertilizer and soil amendments without the work or expense. When I reduce existing lawn areas, I leave the sod in place and kill if off by smothering it with layers of paper or dense mulches. There's no need to go through all of the work to remove sod and haul it off somewhere when the sod decomposes under the mulch and leaves an additional rich mulch layer of its own.

When removing shrubs and trees, cut them off flush with the ground. Any new shoots that appear can be cut off with your weed whacker periodically over the next season to kill off the root.

Create the path by placing steppers on top of paper or cardboard.

Fast and Easy Mulched Path

Some people dig out grass to place stepping stones and this may be appropriate if you want to place steppers across a lawn area. For garden areas, simply lay steppers where you want them and mulch up to them. You avoid the work of digging and you're able to leave 2" (5cm) of space for mulch.

STEP-BY-STEP INSTRUCTIONS

1. Level and smooth the area where the path will go.
2. Apply soil or sand to low areas.
3. Use a flat shovel to scrape down the high areas.
4. Rake as needed.
5. Cover lawn or garden area where path will go with paper or cardboard.
6. Place stepper stones or paver blocks on top of the paper.

You can and should use newspaper, magazines, cardboard or Eco-Weed Barrier™ (a heavy kraft paper) under mulch as a weed barrier. This biodegradable weed barrier will smother most grasses and weeds and keep weed seeds near the surface from sprouting before the weed barrier naturally decomposes. I never use synthetic woven weed barriers because it restricts plant growth, creates shallow roots and is a lot of work to remove later on.

SUPPLIES

**Newspapers,
  Eco-Weed Barrier™,
  or sheets of cardboard**
**Stepping stones or
  paver blocks**
Mulch

TOOLS

Mulch fork
Scissors or utility knife
Wheelbarrow or cart

Adjust spacing for pavers the length of stride for the users.

A mulch or silage fork and a two-wheel wheelbarrow makes for fast mulching.

7. Set the spacing based on how you or other users will walk on this path.
8. Bring out the whole family and have them try walking on the path.
9. Adjust spacing as needed or required by the amount of nagging you receive.
10. Shovel on the mulch.
11. Sweep excess mulch off the steppers.

Don't worry about getting mulch on the steppers.

Finish mulching.

Sweep or rake mulch off the steppers.

You are done! Admire your work.

Just-cut green branches are best because they will compress easier.

A piece of old discarded plywood works fine.

Place the plywood on top of the pile.

Push down so the plywood stays where you put it.

Sticks and Branches Mulch

SUPPLIES

Twigs and branches
Old boards or sheet
  of plywood
Bricks or other weights

TOOLS

Just you

I don't own a chipper. A chipper is a machine that you feed branches into to turn them into wood chips. Commercial chippers are the big, loud and nasty machines that I spent countless hours behind as a municipal arborist. The one I used had a bar that you would trip if the machine accidentally started sucking you in. Obviously the machine never harmed me, but from time to time a stick that was going through the chipper would snag someone's gloves and run those through the machine. If you need a big chipper, hire a tree care company that has one to do it for you. Small homeowner chippers are not worth the time and effort. They are slow and only handle small branches. One day, I heard my neighbor yell to his wife, "Melissa get the fire extinguisher!" A branch had lodged in his small chipper and stopped the cutting wheel, but the engine kept running until the belt caught fire and the machine started burning. There are easier, quieter and less smoky ways to mulch branches.

Take your pile of sticks and branches and weight them down so they are in contact with the soil to hasten their decomposition. You can add grass clippings or leaves to make the process happen faster. Boards or an old piece of plywood weighted down with bricks works fine to press the branches. But why use bricks when you can use that teenager in your house who's sleeping on the sofa right now?

STEP-BY-STEP INSTRUCTIONS

1. Pile branches or sticks where you want to mulch.
2. Place plywood on top of pile.

Carefully step on top to compress sticks.

Place bricks or weights on top.

Leave the pile alone for several weeks so that the sticks settle and compress.

You can remove the plywood when the sticks have dried into the flattened position.

After two years, this area can be worked for gardening or planting.

Mice have assisted by gnawing the branches and fertilizing at the same time. You may not want to do this type of mulching where poisonous snakes are present.

3. Place bricks or weights on top of plywood.
4. Leave alone for three weeks or more.
5. Remove weights and plywood.
6. Add additional mulch over the top.
7. Keep moist to speed decomposition.
8. Leave alone for two years or however long it takes for sticks to decompose.

Weedy areas in existing mulch can be mulched again to remove weeds.

Don't worry about thickness of paper. Thicker is better.

Make sure no weeds show through.

Quick, put the mulch on before the wind blows again.

Large sheets of cardboard are easier to use, if you can get them.

Finish covering with mulch.

Easy Weed Smothering

This is a great project because you won't be rushed to get the plants in. By mulching first, the ideal conditions for growth are created for your new plants. If you run out of time, the mulched area will maintain moisture and prohibit weed growth until you have time to get back.

STEP-BY-STEP INSTRUCTION

1. Use mower or trimmer to cut down tall weeds and grass.
2. Place papers or cardboard on top of weedy areas. Do this a little at a time if it is windy.
3. Make sure the entire surface is completely covered so that no weeds are poking through.
4. Place mulch over paper or cardboard.
5. You are done. Relax.

SUPPLIES

Newspapers, magazines, kraft paper or cardboard
Mulch material

TOOLS

Wheelbarrow
Mulch fork
Scissors or knife

Complete one area and move to the next.

To plant, push back mulch.

Cut out paper or cardboard.

Dig hole.

Install plant.

Bring mulch back up around plant.

6. Plant immediately, or wait a couple of weeks if the original area was very weedy.
7. Pull back mulch where you want to place a plant.
8. Don't be alarmed if after a couple of weeks the paper or cardboard has started to break down.
9. Cut a hole through the cardboard or paper if necessary.
10. Dig a hole for the plant placing extra soil into a wheelbarrow, not on top of the mulch.
11. Place the plant in hole and backfill using extra soil.
12. Continue steps 7 to 11 until you are done.
13. Leftover soil can be used in another place so as not to spread weed seeds on the newly mulched area.
14. If weedy areas re-appear, or if you want to smother weeds in an established landscape, repeat steps 1 to 4.
15. Avoid tilling or pulling weeds in mulched areas. Disturbing the soil surface can result in the right conditions for weed growth.

Any household papers and paper towels can be mulched.

Sprinkle mulch over the top.

Pack it down or let it settle on its own.

PLANTS THAT MAKE MULCH

Many areas of the landscape can be managed to create your own leaf and woody mulch. Rake or sweep tree and shrub leaves back into mulched areas to create another layer of nutritious mulch. Leave pine needles where they fall too. Perennials that die back at the end of the season can be chopped up in place for mulch. Even your vegetable garden can be self-mulching by cutting and breaking up plant debris at the end of the season.

Many deciduous shrubs in cold climates and many plants in warm climates can be cut back and left for mulch with the "chop-and-drop method." They will re-grow and can be chopped back indefinitely.

ADDING PLANTS TO SELF-MULCH AREAS

Mulches and composts are not intended as a visual component of good landscape design. I am seeing more artificially colored (and toxic?) mulches on homeowners' properties, including an entire yard proclaiming pride in the colors of a favorite football team. Yikes! This is even more atrocious and tacky than some holiday light displays. Some people work very hard to reduce the value and look of their property.

You have heard that nature abhors a vacuum. A large mulched area with only a few plants in it is not good design and nature will take the opportunity to fill the space. You will be left to fight off all of the things that will want to grow there and you will be mulching the area yearly to keep it looking good. There are two ways that you can choose to reduce the necessity to re-mulch landscaped areas.

Mulching lawn mowers can be used to trim
ground covers for a neater appearance.

Use mulching lawn mowers for fall or
spring cleanup of ground covers.

Weed whips, weed whackers or string trimmers, as
they are called, can be used to trim ground covers.

Weeds that poke up above the ground cover
can also be trimmed off at the same time.

GROW GROUND COVER PLANTS

There are thousands of ground cover plants that can be placed between large plants in your landscape to fill in bare areas, discourage weeds and reduce the need to re-mulch. In my climate, sun-loving ground covers include lemon thyme, strawberry varieties, prairie smoke, sedum varieties, moss phlox and creeping junipers. Pachysandra, native and European ginger, Canada anemone and sweet woodruff are just a few of the ground covers for shade areas. Sweet potato is also used as a ground cover in tropical areas of the world. With so many ground cover plants available, you're sure to find one, or several, that will be best for your particular situation. Many ground covers can be mowed or trimmed with a weed whacker if you like a neater appearance.

Mulch down a shrub with a manual hedge trimmer. Shown: Dwarf artic willow.

Hmmm. This is taking too long!

Do it faster with a power hedge trimmer.

Now we're making progress.

Almost there.

The stems got too thick for the power hedge trimmer.

Chop-and-Drop Mulching Method

STEP-BY-STEP INSTRUCTIONS

1. First, check with your spouse or partner so that you don't cut down their favorite rose that is about to blossom.
2. Seriously, read up on the plants you are planning to cut back. Some will do better if cut down during certain times of the year.
3. Cut off stems in as short a section as possible.
4. Continue cutting. If stems become too big for the tool you are using, switch to a bigger tool.
5. Cut all the way to the base of the plant, if you desire.
6. You have just completed mulching the area around that plant.
7. Do it again next season.

SUPPLIES

Plants you are already growing

TOOLS

Manual hedge shears, electric or gas hedge shears, gas brush saw, machete, chain saw, brush hook or other tools of destruction.

Rent a gas brush saw. They are easy and safe to use.

The brush saw made quick work of the thick stems.

Brush-saw blades are replaceable and can be sharpened.

Shrub reduced to mulch.

For a neater appearance, add a little top dressing of another mulch.

This red-stem dogwood put on over two feet (61cm) of growth in one season after being cut back with a chain saw.

Large dogwood stems can be set aside as fuel for heating or cooking.

Benefits of Projects for Easy-Going Personalities

FAST AND EASY MULCHED PATH

You'll be amazed at the benefits to creating a path this way:
- Takes one-tenth the time of traditional path construction.
- No digging to set path stones.
- Existing grass or weeds can be smothered with free paper or cardboard.
- No measuring required.
- Everyone in the family can participate in the project.

STICKS AND BRANCHES MULCH PROJECT

Take advantage of these benefits to sticks and branches mulch:
- No power equipment needed.
- Quiet and clean.
- No gas or oil fumes.
- No turning of compost or mulch required.
- Safe for children and adults.

EASY WEED SMOTHERING PROJECT

Here are the benefits to easy weed smothering:
- Doesn't require using herbicides.
- Uses free paper, junk mail or cardboard.
- Increase soil fertility while getting rid of the weeds.
- Increases the amount of earthworms and other beneficial organisms.
- Plant immediately or wait; it's your choice.
- Reduces erosion and soil loss.
- Holds moisture for better growing conditions.

CHOP-AND-DROP MULCHING METHOD

You will never look at plants the same after seeing the benefits to chop-and-drop mulching:
- No need to pick up clippings from shrub trimming (which is the job I hate the most).
- Free mulch material.
- Rejuvenates shrubs and perennials fast and easy.
- Uses existing tools you already own.
- Reduces erosion and moisture loss.
- Adds needed nutrients and organic material to your soil.

Plants for the Easy-Going Personality

If you identify yourself as having a peaceful and easy-going personality, you're in luck. You will have the easiest time of all personalities finding plants that fit your style. When choosing plants, keep in mind that they should be low maintenance and not a hassle to take care of. You will not want any (or only a few) high-maintenance plants like highbred roses or fussy orchids.

GROUND COVER PLANTS

Ground cover plants of all varieties help reduce lawn area and mulched areas between existing plants. Once planted, ground covers expand and fill the area and require little care. This sure beats cutting the whole lawn every week or putting new mulch down around plants every year. Ground cover plants that take the place of lawn and mulch can be trimmed with a mower once or twice a year if you want a neater appearance. There are many ground cover plants for every climate. In warm climates, sweet potatoes can be used as a perennial ground cover with the bonus of edible tubers.

VINES

People with your personality should not overlook the many types of vines available. Vines can be used to create screening and privacy by placing them on an arbor creating a truly private place to sit and reflect. Vines, like grapes, can give you that old-world charm or the laid back California look. Vines can make ugly or stark walls inviting. Add a little water feature and slip into a whole other world after work.

EASY-GOING PLANTS TO GO EASY ON THE ENVIRONMENT

Using ground cover plants will reduce mowed lawn areas and reduce pesticide use in plant beds. Using the chop-and-drop method of pruning shrubs is easy for you and reduces the use of fossil fuels to transport waste out or bring new mulch in. Trees, shrubs and vines used for privacy also provide shade and windbreaks, so they reduce your cooling and heating demands for your home and that's good for the environment. Edible plants that are part of your landscape reduce your need to purchase from the store, help you eat healthier and save you money on fossil fuels and time.

Chapter 12
Put Water to Work for You

If you want to create all sorts of benefits from all of the free water that falls on your property, this is the chapter you've been looking for. I am going to show you how water that falls from precipitation can be used repeatedly to create multiple benefits on your property.

Water from precipitation and the soil on your property are the most important resources you can have. Surprisingly, these two features are even more valuable than your home. Without water, your soil is of limited value. Properly used and managed water on your property will create an excess of benefits from the soil. Previous chapters have shown how to take advantage of other resources to improve soil and growing conditions. This chapter will help you use water in better ways.

My property contains contour swales, off-grade swales, dug ponds, ponds with liners, wetlands, small and large tank water storage, drip irrigation, micro-irrigation, irrigation controls and pumps and plumbing for transporting water. You get to choose the features that take advantage of the water on your own property.

For practical use of water on your property, choose methods that actually will work for you. Supposedly enlightened gardening speakers, gardening groups and extension services are advocating rain barrels and rain gardens and are quite hostile toward my view, dismissing it as impractical. For many, but not all people, rain barrels and rain gardens are not useful and terribly inefficient. It reminds me of the phrase often recited by my English grandmother, "penny wise and pound foolish." Many properties are wasting and polluting hundreds of thousands of gallons of water yearly. A puny rain barrel that is used for a few gallons of water a week is insignificant. Rain barrels and rain gardens are the biggest waster of time, money and water for people looking to benefit from a sustainable landscape. You can only create true benefits for yourself when you have an efficient system. Getting bogged down with the latest gadget or fad in water conservation just creates greater dependency on purchasing the water you need. There are many easier, better, and more sustainable ways to use all that free water that falls on your home and yard and I'm going to tell you about the ones that work.

OUR WATER DILEMMA

All over the world, a poor job is being done using, saving, and benefiting from water. It is more obvious in the United States than elsewhere because we changed and altered the landscape and cheated ourselves out of great water resources in less than 100 years. Other places on the planet have had thousands of years to muck-up water and still can't aspire to our level of incompetence with water resources.

Our land uses decide how much water we will have, where it will go and whether we will benefit from water or just view it as a problem.

- It is generally accepted that 50 to 85 percent of wetlands in the U.S. have been drained or filled for agriculture and development since white settlement.
- Nearly 100 percent of city and suburban housing lots have been altered to remove ephemeral wetlands and to increase the rate of precipitation run-off.
- A variety of sources and studies show a decline in flora and fauna related to a decline in water quality and wetland losses.
- Increased flooding of homes and businesses is being seen more frequently, not only in coastal areas and flood plains, but in places never flooded before because water is not being allowed to absorb into the ground where it falls.
- At the same time, an increase in fires at the parched interface of wild lands and urban areas is occurring more often because water is allowed to run off too rapidly.

Isn't that interesting? Flooding and drought have become more of a man-made event than natural occurrences and both are related to moving water, too fast, from one place to another. Most problems that we face in the environment either impact water or are caused by the way we treat water. You can change this situation by altering the way you use water where you live.

In most traditional landscapes, the focus has been to move water off the property as fast as possible. By removing organic materials, natural plant communities and natural mulches, water from melted snow or rain runs off more rapidly. Natural woodlands and native grasslands had plant structures, root systems, organic debris and specialized plant communities adapted to slow water movement with the intent to use it. Wetlands, lakes, streams and rivers had natural-occurring features that slowed water down, absorbed it, or let it spread out harmlessly. These natural buffers that slow the travel of precipitation no longer exist as they once did. You can put back natural features in your yard that will help replace what has been lost. Putting back these features will result in reducing lawn area that you really aren't using anyway.

REDUCING LAWN AREAS TO REDUCE WATER USE

Lawn areas are not good at absorbing heavy rains. The resulting run-off containing fertilizers, pesticides and pet wastes often ends up polluting nearby streams and lakes and ultimately your drinking water.

There are now about 40 million acres of lawn in the U.S. Lawn grasses here are not native, not even Kentucky bluegrass. Lawns are the largest irrigated crop in the country and even surpass corn (maize) acreage. Irrigation of lawns accounts for 40 to 80 percent of water used (wasted) in city and suburban residential areas.

Local water and utility companies have a vested interest in this extreme water use. A common practice for utility companies in many areas is to charge you less per unit for using more water. The more water you use, the more money the utility makes. The trouble with this is that the more water the utility companies pump, the more it draws water from a larger area and with that comes more pollutants. The property owner is caught in an upward spiral of water costs as more time, equipment and chemicals are used to purify the water that continues to decline in quality. This situation is not any better if you have a private well. In many places, private wells are drying up as the water table drops because of pumping more water out than is being replaced. Your private well may not be far from a septic system. The more water you pump out of your private well, the better chance that chemicals, nutrients and viruses from yours' and your neighbor's septic system end up in your water.

Reducing lawn areas will reduce your long-term maintenance costs and significantly reduce your need for pumping water for irrigation out of the ground. Most lawn grasses are "cool season" grasses and require a great deal of water to maintain them. In my climate, a quarter-acre (0.1ha) lawn with a sprinkler system uses about 80,000 gallons (3,637hl) of water in just 12 weeks. A one-acre (0.4ha) lot uses a whopping 320,000 gallons (14,547hl) of water in the same amount of time. You will benefit by using rainwater on your property, but it would be very difficult to irrigate a large lawn with rainwater because of the amount of water storage required. Large lawns are just not suited to most of the climates they are grown in. Replacing unused lawn areas with desirable vegetation suited to the growing conditions on your property can significantly reduce water needs.

WATER USE IN THE HOME

It always amazes me that we are required to have low-flow shower-heads, low-flush toilets and even low-flow faucets for kitchens, yet all that conservation literally goes out the door when it comes to water conservation for our lawns and landscapes. While we are using more water in our landscapes than ever before, we are using less in our homes. The average person in their home now uses about 40 gallons (151L) of water a day, down from 60 gallons (227 L) prior to household water conservation measures. Less than one gallon (4L) of water a day per person is consumed as drinking water.

Much of the water used in our homes is simply to transport waste. Our culture's fascination with flush toilets results in two gallons (8L) of perfectly clean water used to transport a few ounces of waste multiple times a day. Many people find they need to flush water-saving toilets twice and then end up using more water than standard toilets. Our septic and sewage systems treat bacteria in the waste, but often do nothing to keep nutrients out of the ground and surface waters.

In most places, people don't have the luxury of polluting pristine water like we do. They would be happy with water that is as clean as the water going down our sink and shower drains. About 80 percent of the world's population uses untreated water that is not much cleaner than our used household water prior to sewage treatment for all their daily purposes.

Most pharmaceuticals from human waste have now reached detectable levels in rivers, oceans and groundwater. Whole aquifers are drying up because water pumped out in one area is piped into and used in another. Now, there are plans to pump sewage water back into the ground upstream to replenish these aquifers. That's right, you are drinking the combined experience that your water has been through. All the nutrients, pesticides, drugs and cleaning chemicals that you use on a daily basis come right back to you in every beverage you drink.

The worst part of our water mismanagement is that we are not achieving the benefits that we could derive from our water use. Imagine having all of the free water you could ever use, using the same water several times on your own property, creating things of value with it, growing food, having fun and then returning it to the environment cleaner and better than when you first got it — Let's get started!

WATER AND YOUR LIFESTYLE

Before I get started discussing efficient use of water on your property — Guess what? Yes, water use must fit your current lifestyle, the lifestyle you desire and your personality. In previous chapters, I have shown many examples of projects that fit different lifestyles and personalities, and water use is no different.

The reason many people's rain barrels overflow and their rain gardens turn into weedy holes is because, not only are they inefficient, they also were not specifically designed for an individual's lifestyle. Rain barrels and rain gardens don't produce the benefits expected and end up being neglected. Here are some basic questions that need to be addressed before you begin:

- Where and how will your water be used? While this seems like a simple question, no two people will have the exact same answer.
- Do you want to make something fun like an outdoor shower?
- Are you looking to hear the peaceful sound of a gurgling waterfall?
- Do you want to have more control over the water you use?
- Do you want a precise flow of water using drip irrigation?
- How does the water that falls on your property fit into your lifestyle?
- Will you use pumps and piping to move the water? Most people don't have enough time or physical ability to carry buckets of water all over their property.
- How will you store precipitation?
- Do you want a very low-maintenance system?
- How precise does the application of water need to be?
- Can the water have some debris and pollutants in it or does it need to be crystal clear and safe for drinking?
- Do you need water at specific times of the day?

Make a list of all of the things on your property where you would like to use water and determine if your needs can be met by managing rainfall and snowmelt that are free for the using. When water use fits your lifestyle, you will have more time to do what you want, you'll actually use less water, and you will create more benefits for yourself. The water you return to the environment will be cleaner and healthier for you, your neighbor, and the next person downstream.

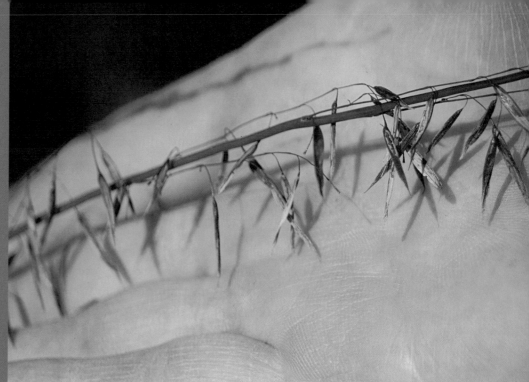

In my climate, wild rice is one of the plants that grows well in wet areas. What can you grow?

WATER WITH BENEFITS

You can take better advantage of water benefits if you know how physical forces affect water. Some great things to remember for sustainable water use:

- Keep water as high up on your property as you can. Water will naturally move downhill or down slope. Moving water uphill requires energy input. The longer it takes water to move downhill, the more opportunities you have to use it multiple times.
- Very few properties are perfectly flat; yours probably has some slope. You don't need much slope to get water to flow where you want it.
- For every 2.33 feet (71cm) that you raise water, it will exert one psi (7kPa) (pound of pressure per square inch). This is why water towers are so tall and why you want to take advantage of as much height in gravity-fed applications as possible.
- There is a limit to height in gravity-fed applications. Piping water down from a 400-foot (122m) elevation would give you a pressure of over 170 psi. (1,172kPa). That's a fire hose! Can you and your plumbing handle that?
- Allowing water to fill holding areas, or non-pressurized tanks placed periodically on slopes, will reduce its pressure in piping to only the height of the previous tank.

Switch grass grows in a variety of places, as it tolerates very dry or very wet conditions.

- Water that is stopped on slopes by holding areas, tanks or swales will only have the erosion energy that it can build up for that segment of the slope. You can greatly reduce erosion by briefly stopping water and then allowing it to resume its journey.
- The longer water is held on your property, the more water that will be absorbed by the soil. The more water that is absorbed by the soil, the longer you will have moisture available to plants and other uses between rainfalls.
- Areas of your property that are wet now should not be drained. Take advantage of these areas for what they offer. I grow wild rice, cranberries, decorative willows, native wetland plants and a variety of tree species for firewood in my wetland areas. What will you do with the wet area on your property?
- Resist the urge to trench, channel or straighten excavations to move water faster. Doing so has the potential of creating erosion.
- Slow the pace of water on hillsides by leaving natural features, including fallen trees, leaves and needles.

CATCH THE WAVE

Use all surfaces on your property to collect and use precipitation. Roofs, driveways and patios, and the ground surface itself, all provide water catchments and transport. It takes a lot of time and energy to pump, move and distribute water. In a sustainable landscape, you want to create landform changes to let the water work for you and create benefits without extra work.

In Chapter 9, I showed you how to construct an outdoor shower. Used water from the shower flows right to the plants that need watering. This is an example where water is used for two purposes. There are some additional secondary benefits from this particular situation, including less heat and humidity in the house during summer, air-drying towels outside and less bathroom cleaning. As you use water, look for all of the benefits you can reap from it.

ROOF MATERIALS

Roof materials make a difference in water collection and how the water is used. Metal, slate, tile and untreated wood shingle roofs will produce very high-quality water from rain. Many parts of the world use roof water with minimal filtering and treatment from these types of roofs for all applications, including irrigation and drinking water. Water run-off from asphalt-shingled roofs (popular in the United States) contains a small amount of hydrocarbon contaminants, but it's suitable for irrigation. Unpainted, galvanized metal roofs can release a small amount of zinc with each rainfall. Zinc sulfate in this small amount is not toxic to people, but can damage lower life forms, including, but not limited to, moss, lichens, fish and other aquatic animals at just 10 parts per billion.

There are concerns among some that rainwater and roof water are not safe and/or it's seriously polluted. Where you live, it may be possible that high air pollution levels make rainfall dangerous, but what is the alternative? Rainfall becomes groundwater and surface water that then is pumped and distributed as drinking water!

There is an additional concern that roof water may contain harmful bacteria from bird droppings and should not be used on vegetable crops. This is a housekeeping issue and involves periodically cleaning gutters and diverting the initial "first flush" of rain coming off the roof to another use. If you have a lot of bird droppings, think of it as liquid fertilizer!

GUTTERS, VALLEYS AND EAVES

Your home may already have gutters to channel water off the roof and away from the house. From a one-inch (2.5cm) rainfall, the average home easily can produce 1,000 gallons (38hl) or more of water from roof diversion. You can channel all of that water to a variety of structures in your landscape for immediate use or holding. If you do not have gutters, but you do have valleys (where two roofs intersect) concentrate on using the water that runs off from the valley because of the large volume. Homes without gutters or valleys still can collect the water below the eaves and channel it to areas where it is needed. In some climates, rain gutters don't work well and the area below the roof eaves easily can be altered to channel and move water. My home and outbuildings take advantage of gutters, valleys and eaves. I use my gutters to transport the highest quality water on my property to a large tank. Roof valleys provide water for some small pond areas and eaves directly water some plants. Because I have metal roofs, some condensation is collected every morning by gutters, valleys and eaves and this also is used.

DRIVEWAYS, PATIOS AND OTHER IMPERVIOUS SURFACES

You probably have areas on your property where rain runs off and doesn't get used. Sometimes, these solid surfaces can cause excessive amounts of rainfall to collect in the wrong spot, cause erosion or even run into your basement or garage and create flooding problems. Driveways and patios can be constructed or retrofitted to produce a benefit by providing a means for collecting water.

Most residential, small patios and parking areas can be tapered and slanted so that rain is collected in one area and allowed to be moved via a shallow swale. Large driveways and parking lots need to be properly designed so that rainfall does not erode soils along the edges — leave this to the experts. Some designers tend to run all of the water off a parking lot in only one or two areas. This essentially could create a flash flood from tens of thousands of gallons of water. It is better to break up large impervious surfaces into smaller drainage units if you want to benefit from the use of this water.

Common problems for homeowners are driveways that are higher at the road and lower by the garage. Water runs down the driveway and into the garage, or worse yet, the house. Landscaping activities that raise the soil level along the edges of the driveway exacerbate this problem. For existing paved driveways, add trench drains at regular intervals, perpendicular to the drive, to catch water and divert it to shallow swales leading away from the driveway. Trench drains resemble rain gutters and are installed by cutting the pavement, installing the gutter, and placing a slotted cover on the top. For new driveways, trench drains can be installed when the paving is installed. Periodic placement of several trench drains along the driveway may be important because of the large surface area and energy present from the water running downhill.

Using a shovel, you can dig a swale like the one shown. This swale is located on a slope above a pond. Mulched with cattails, it slows the water flow and reduces erosion, provides water to plants in the bottom of the swale, and filters the water as it flows to the pond.

There are a variety of structures to store and use the water you have collected from land surfaces, roofs and other impervious surfaces.

SWALES

Swales are simply shallow depressions that hold water or move it to another location. For some homes with yards that have very little slope, I have used swales less than six inches (15cm) deep to move water away from the house and deposit it in planting areas. Swales need very little slope and it is OK for some water to sit in them for a few hours after a rainfall. You can dig these types of swales with a shovel and they can be shallow enough that they may not be visible to most people looking at the landscape.

Swales can be made level too, and this type of land feature is designed to slow run-off so it can be absorbed into the soil. These are called contour swales because they follow the contour of the land and are perpendicular to the slope at all locations. Contour swales are similar to the practice of contour plowing except there is undisturbed space above and below each swale. A contour swale can be a shallow shovel-dug trench or a massive cut made with a bulldozer. The size of the swale is dependant on the amount of water it will hold back, soil conditions and intended purposes. These shallow indentations allow water to soak into the ground.

Plants can be placed just below the excavation in the bottom of the swale, or above it, depending on the type of soil and the moisture requirements of the plants. On substantial slopes, swales may be placed consecutively down the grade and may need engineering. Level spillways also may need to be engineered into swales on substantial slopes so that there is a place for water to overflow without eroding the original excavation. Level spillways allow a very thin sheet of water to pass over them so that the erosive energy in the water is dissipated. Then, the water is allowed to move down to the next swale or holding structure.

There are areas throughout the world where contour swales have flushed surface salts from the soil on slopes and allowed these slopes to be re-vegetated after being severely damaged by agricultural activities. You also can combine swales with snow fences to create and store snowdrifts, which then slowly melt and transport that water for use.

A pond like this provides many benefits and holds spring rains and run-off for months.

PONDS

A pond can be a great water-holding feature for your property. It requires some thought and planning prior to construction, but you'll gain many benefits.

PONDS WITHOUT SYNTHETIC LINERS

There are two types of ponds that you can build without synthetic liners — a pond dug into an area with a high water table and a pond dug into clay soils that holds water.

Many people are under the impression that ponds are "spring-fed." While some are, most ponds are simply dug into an existing water table or filled by run-off from the surrounding property.

Ponds constructed where there is a high water table can be very small or lake-size. The surface of the pond will be equal to the height of the existing water table. Ponds constructed in clay soils resemble a clay pot. Water slowly moves through the clay and the pond is filled by natural precipitation and run-off. In both types of ponds, there may be seasonal changes in water depth.

Proper planning, permitting, and design are all things to be considered when building a pond. Many people lease equipment and just dig a hole in the ground. Then, they wonder why they have erosion, undesirable aquatic plants, pests, and poor water quality. Soil tests need to be done to determine water table levels. It also is important to test clay soils to make sure there are no veins of sand or rock that essentially would drain this type of pond.

How you use your pond is important. Can it support fish? Will you swim in it? Do you plan to use the pond to hold irrigation water? What are your expectations of water quality? What land features will you construct to reduce erosion and nutrient inputs? Can you maintain the pond the way you want without costly and dangerous pesticides?

You should employ a soil scientist, a hydrologist and a sustainable landscape specialist to assist you with testing and advice. In addition, there may be a variety of government agencies that you need to contact for permits relating to pond construction.

If you have clay deposits on your property, line the pond with clay to hold water. The thicker the clay liner, the better the pond will retain water. Small dams also can be built out of clay.

Use erosion control materials, like this coconut fiber log, to protect the edges of newly dug ponds.

There are many decisions you need to make prior to the start of pond construction, but it will be worth the effort. The dug pond on my property provides me with all sorts of benefits, including a place for kids to fish (and actually catch fish) a supply of irrigation water, wildlife viewing, emergency use for fire fighting, aquatic plants that are cut for mulches and a way to hold back and slowly use a large volume of water.

Native wetland shrubs and trees like these willows with mat-forming roots help protect shorelines.

Building and maintaining a natural-looking pond like this is easier than a more formal-looking water feature.

PONDS WITH SYNTHETIC LINERS

If you don't have a high water table or clay soil you still can have a pond on your property by using a synthetic liner.

There is a large amount of information available in books and on the Internet to learn how to construct ponds with synthetic liners. So, I'm only going to tell you what these sources often don't mention. Things to keep in mind when constructing a synthetic-lined pond:

- Don't believe claims that somehow, you are going to be creating a balanced ecosystem with your pond. People don't create balanced ecosystems; nature does, and you may not be happy with what nature thinks is "balanced."
- There are all sorts of liners available, some with long warranties. What is a warranty worth if it only covers the cost for the liner, but not the 100 hours of labor to replace it? Liners range from cheap thin plastic to substantially thick synthetic rubber. You get what you pay for here.
- Shallow ponds in cold climates will freeze all the way to the bottom. Fish will die in this sort of situation, and you can expect to see dead frogs too. These types of ponds usually are not set up to accommodate winter hibernation of frogs. Lowering the water in the pond before winter is a good way to get frogs to migrate to safer places to hibernate.
- Pesticides, algaecides and other chemicals labeled "safe" for ponds are not! Why would you put a pesticide in 1,000 gallons (38hl) of water that will be in contact with wildlife, children and pets?
- If you want crystal clear water to look at, build a swimming pool instead. Managing water quality in small ponds is very difficult. It changes with the season, temperature, water chemistry, rainfall, phase of the moon and just about everything else you can imagine.
- Plant your pond with as many aquatic plants as possible. This provides a habitat for many desirable species, and it breaks up the view of the water so that you see less algae.
- You don't need to buy rich soils to grow the aquatic plants. You can plant most water-loving plants in sand or small gravel, as they will use the nutrients from the pond water.
- Filters, pumps, plumbing and other features are expensive, have to be replaced, and their use can substantially raise your utility bill. Plan your pond in advance with realistic budgetary goals and maintenance costs. Place waterfalls on timers or motion-sensors so that they are only using power when you desire.
- Don't place bird feeders that attract rodents near your lined pond. You guessed right! Rodents chew on plumbing and through liners.
- Many people who raise ornamental fish end up with too many in their pond. Pick a fish variety that you wouldn't mind eating to create another benefit from your pond. Frog legs anyone?

A pond skimmer removes algae from small ponds. Algaecides cause string algae to die and sink to the bottom of the pond and harm the environment.

Manually remove the algae. You won't have to use pesticides, and you deter the nutrients that cause algae growth. Algae works great as a mulch around plants too.

I really enjoy my lined pond. Nestled near our patio, the waterfall sound drowns out noise in the neighborhood and we get to see dragonflies, frogs, and birds in a close and personal way. We don't use pesticides in our pond and the maintenance is minimal. We have a very efficient pump that is used only when we are enjoying the pond and the soft, low-voltage lighting adds to our use and enjoyment.

Many people contemplating a pond are concerned about creating mosquito-breeding areas. With several pond areas on our property, and proper habitat, we now have fewer mosquitoes than when our property was just an alfalfa field. Because we don't use pesticides, our ponds actually are mosquito larvae traps. Mosquitoes lay their eggs in the water and our frogs and dragonflies eat the larvae. Insect-eating birds and bats drawn to these same habitats also eat many of the mosquitoes. You can create your own mosquito-trapping ponds through proper design and help from sustainable pond experts.

Dragonflies, damselflies and other beneficial insects control mosquitoes when you don't use pesticides in your pond.

WATER TANKS

Water tanks can be built or installed on your property for storing water. They also are the most expensive way to store water. If you have very limited space, or if you live in an arid climate where evaporation and water cost is significant, you'll want to store only your best-quality water in a tank.

We use a 2,500-gallon (95hl) tank for storing roof water for our outdoor shower, emergency irrigation, water for our chickens and to pipe into the house when our well does not work. You can use a solar-powered pump (see page 69) to move water from a tank, such as this, if gravity will not do the work for you. Our tank is only supplemental for potable water and would not meet our daily needs alone. Our tank produces additional benefits by forming the north wall of the chicken coop which helps warm the chicken coop during the winter and cool it during the summer. Happy chickens lay more eggs!

You will need about one inch (2.5cm) of rain for each 1,000 gallons (38hl) of rainwater collected from your house roof if all of the gutters and downspouts are attached to your tank. Your climate and needs will guide you in determining your tank size. In an arid climate with sporadic rainfall, or a cold climate where freezing prevents water collection, a 10,000-to 20,000-gallon (378hl to 757hl) tank may be needed to supply all of your household water needs.

There are many articles and books available on building, using and siting water tanks. Much of this information comes from climates with limited groundwater resources and can be applied to wherever you live. There are ways to automatically flush your roof before water goes into the tank, ways to change the pH of the water, and ways to filter it, if needed. You can create water storage that is efficient, safe and beneficial to you by researching the existing information and getting help from experts in this area.

PUTTING IT ALL TOGETHER

Now that you have all the parts for efficient water use, let's put them together!

Roofs and other surfaces form a collection surface for precipitation. Gutters, downspouts, pipes, and trench drains and swales gather up the water in quantity. From there, water can be directed into sloped swales for further transport or fed directly into ponds or tanks. Ponds or tanks that are elevated over other parts of the property, or equipped with pumps, can in turn be a source of water fed through swales or pipes for a variety of uses. Contour swales can hold water on hillsides and slowly release that water to lower swales, tanks or ponds. Through the whole process of slowing moving water through your property, the same water is used over and over again. A portion is

*It **is** easy being green when you have all of the clean water you want!*

absorbed into the soil, some water is going to strategically located plants or crops, some is being withdrawn to use in other locations, and still other water is benefiting wildlife.

Does it seem greedy to use all this water? Well, it isn't. Not only are you returning high-quality water back to nature, but your neighbor downstream benefits too. Because of your careful water management, your down-slope neighbors will be getting more usable and better quality water because of you. Available water downstream of your property increases during dry periods because of the things you have done to slow the water flow by weeks or months instead of letting it pass through in days or hours. You also protect your neighbor and yourself from damaging floods. Remember, no one needs water when it's raining — they need it when it's not.

Chapter 13

Top 10 Must-Have Items for Creating Your Eco-Friendly Yard

Your home and landscape are intertwined in shared benefits. I want to share with you the most basic things that have made my lifestyle a true joy. Pay close attention to the first four: heat, water, food and love. Does this sound like some basic things you'd want to have?

THE MASONRY HEATER

The Chinese call them *kangs* and in Germany they are called *kachelofen* (tile oven). If you live in a climate where heating is needed, then you can choose the most efficient way to heat your home too. Masonry heaters, as they are known here, are safe, clean, miserly with fuel and comfortable. With my training, education and knowledge in forestry, it is easy for me to recommend the practice of clean-burning wood for home heating and cooking wherever wood is in plentiful supply and where solar heating is not enough. Unfortunately, many people in my area of the country are choosing outdoor wood boilers for home heating. Most of these boilers, but not all, are extremely inefficient, burning six or seven times more wood than my masonry heater. Most outside wood boilers are extreme air polluters because wood is not burned at the proper temperature or with the right amount of air. I jokingly recommend that if you are planning on installing an outdoor wood boiler, your whole family, including the kids, should start chain smoking cigarettes because at least you will have a filter between your lungs and the dangerous amount of smoke coming from the outdoor wood boiler. Localized air pollution is no joke. During thermal inversions in cold climates, the smoke from these outdoor wood boilers envelopes the whole neighborhood and seeps into homes. Some municipalities near us have taken this air pollution issue seriously enough to outlaw outdoor wood boilers in their communities.

Our masonry heater has been operated daily during the winter since 1995. We heat about 80 percent of the about 4,500 square feet (418m²) of living, office and storage space on two cords (9m³) of wood a winter. There has been no maintenance and we haven't needed to clean the chimney because of its clean burning characteristics with any kind of wood.

Use clean wood ash from heating and cooking as fertilizer and safe deicer.

To know if you are getting an efficient wood burner, ask if it meets Phase II EPA emissions. Phase II limits are 7.5 grams/hour of particulate emission (smoke) in appliances without catalytic combustors.

I mention home heating because you can use free scrap wood from nearby, or as a way to use waste wood from your own property. Fire starter is the junk mail you already receive and the very clean wood ash from masonry heaters can be used as a sidewalk deicer or as a fertilizer in your landscape. So, as you can see, masonry heaters produce multiple benefits to you and your property. They do so with very small amounts of emissions and do not threaten your safety or health.

LARGE WATER STORAGE

Will your water supply be there when you need it? I'm not going to trust my well or a municipal water supply for water when I need it most. Rainwater is probably the safest water left on the planet. Yes, rain contains pollutants, but every other water supply has more natural and man-made contaminants than rain. If you want to take advantage of all the good-quality free water you could ever have, then harvesting rain is the way to go. Instead of moving water as fast as possible off your property, do all you can to slow it down and take advantage of it. On our property, a 2,500 gallon (95hl) cistern collects the best water for a variety of purposes and could be filtered for drinking. On-grade swales on slopes of our property allow rainfall to slowly soak in, keeping plants moist for long periods of time. A large pond on our property collects run-off and provides water for swimming, fishing and irrigation. Mulched areas soak up rainfall and help maintain soil moisture. In total, low-cost changes to our property are allowing us to use and reuse hundreds of thousands of gallons of water every year without pumping it out of the ground. Benefits are the same whether you live in a wet or dry climate. In a wet climate, these methods reduce erosion, downstream flooding and provide water during dry seasons. In very dry climates, these same techniques can save your crop from failure, bring alkaline soils back to life and prevent flash-flood damage on your property.

One cubic foot of bark mulch will hold one to two gallons (4L to 8L) of water. A cubic meter of mulch could hold as much as 52 gallons (200L) of water.

Apples, raspberries and walking onions are just a few of the perennial food plants that you can grow in a far northern climate.

GROW PERENNIAL FOOD CROPS

Every part of the world has easy-to-grow perennial foods — vegetables, fruits, nuts and root crops. I can't imagine living in a tropical area where sweet potato is viewed as a weed! The reason that you can grow perennial foods easier, faster and cheaper than anything else is because you only have to plant them once. In our climate, asparagus, fruit and nut trees, rhubarb, perennial onions, many herbs, strawberries, blueberries, horseradish, sunchokes and (Wisconsin is famous for beer) hops are some of the perennials I grow. Once planted, perennials need management, but they don't need replanting and that saves you money and time.

SHARE YOUR SUSTAINABLE LIFESTYLE

That someone could be a partner, spouse, children or other family members, friends, people from work, or how about someone not as fortunate as you. One of the key principles of a sustainable landscape is that it frees your time, effort and resources so that you have something to pass on to others. How neat is that? While you are benefiting yourself, you can actually create benefits for others and the environment. Because I only spend about two hours a week maintaining our seven and one-half acres (3ha), I'm able to do a lot of other things, including volunteering time in my community. Who is that special person or persons that you will share and spend time with?

Purslane produces 5,000 to 10,000 seeds the size of finely ground pepper. You are not going to keep these out of your garden anyway so why not eat them?

GROW WEEDS

Yes, you can have weeds as part of your eco-friendly yard and you can benefit from them. Weeds are site indicators, micro-nutrient concentrators, food for wildlife, mulch, soil amendments, companion plants for more desirable vegetation and a great source of nutrition for people. I favor purslane in my garden because it forms an annual ground cover. Purslane can be roasted, eaten raw as a coleslaw alternative and it has more omega-3 than salmon. Mullein, another weed that grows on my property, has a tall flower stalk with seeds that is a natural winter feeder for birds.

Some breeds of chicken, like this Barred Rock, are easy to train.

By using the built-up litter method, you can create great fertilizer from chicken droppings and the chickens do all of the work of turning and breaking up the compost.

RAISE PET CHICKENS

Instead of buying the kids a pet rabbit or a rodent, why not a couple of laying hens? What can you do with a rabbit? You can't eat it, because the kids would freak out. It just sits there in a cage and you feed it until you get sick of it and then what do you do? A pair of laying hens would provide you with about a dozen eggs a week. You wouldn't have to go to the store to buy eggs and the kids would actually get to see where their food comes from. The best thing about chickens is that they are descendants of jungle fowl, and they will eat anything that you give them. I feed ours everything, and I mean everything that we eat, except chicken. Chickens are the ultimate form of recycling. Leftovers, stale bread, shrimp tails and vegetable peels get turned into eggs and great fertilizer. It is not true that chickens are grain eaters. Mine prefer greens to grain in side-by-side tests every time.

Cupplant is native to where we live. Its leaves hold water long after a rain giving birds a place to drink.

CREATE NATURE

You can have a bit of nature with even the smallest property. It is no wonder that so many companies now tout the effectiveness of remedies that contain ingredients from nature. The best thing that children and adults can do is go roll in the dirt of a totally natural area. Concrete and chemically-laced lawns may be outside, but they are not nature. Children without nature to play in are seriously neglected. Create space in your yard for true nature by not killing plants that are coming up, by not using pesticides, by not using fertilizer, by not raking the leaves or needles and by not running power equipment through that area. Yes, you can create a natural area that will offer multiple benefits to you by not doing anything! And then give the kids a shovel and tell them to dig a hole in that area and make a fort!

GIVE NAYSAYERS THE COLD SHOULDER

There are so many things that you can do. Yet, sustainable landscapes are such a revolutionary idea, that many don't even know this option exists. Those that don't understand that you can create benefits from your yard probably won't be supportive of what you are doing. Don't bother trying to convert the non-believers. That will cut into the time you have to accomplish things that really matter to you and your family. You can't create that eco-friendly yard with all of the benefits if you hang around with people that are all consumed with cutting their lawn to the exact millimeter. Don't forget that seeing is believing. My experience is that when people see the success I've had, they emulate it. Take the lead!

You can reduce the use of pesticides, have standing water on your property and have less bothersome insects because dragonflies are great predators of mosquitoes and other flying bugs.

Remember, unless you are the lead dog on a dog-sled team, the view is always the same.

Early spring flowers, like this pasqueflower, add color and interest to your landscape.

MAKE IT FIT YOUR PERSONALITY AND YOUR LIFESTYLE

Up until now, it has been rare to equate landscape with personality and lifestyle, which is why there are so many dysfunctional landscapes out there. I've spent a little time in this book dealing with personality and lifestyle. There is still much to learn in this area. You can do some introspection and analysis with significant others who share your landscape to guide you to do the right thing. It is very difficult for me to listen to what others want because I have really strong opinions. After all, when I got my forestry degree, we were taught to talk to trees not people. But guess what? Plants aren't the most important part of the landscape — people are! So, I'm training myself to get better at listening. You can get better at hearing what others have to say by writing down what they are telling you and then repeating it back to them in your own words. That works wonders and avoids unneeded arguments. When you share the landscape with others, you will find that there are areas in the landscape that can be developed for each personality, and these areas will complement each other. The reason for this is because each one of us is not just one personality. We have one or two strong personality points and then several others that aren't as strong. This means that at different times we might like a variety of things in the landscape, and this is where different personalities can come together to create truly great landscapes that everyone will enjoy.

ACCEPT CHANGE IN YOUR LANDSCAPE

To continue to do things the same way and expect different results is my version of insanity. Your eco-friendly yard will be a change for you. A change for the better. I've had customers defend having a large lawn because "the kids need a place to run around." However, children left to their own devices will seek out natural areas to climb trees, build forts, discover new things, throw rocks in water, hunt for snakes and toads and a whole bunch of other healthy activities not associated with turf. I've also had the experience of meeting with older couples, or those with a spouse who has just passed away, that can no longer take care of the landscape they built when they were younger. Some have been in tears as they admit to me that they can no longer maintain the "monster" landscape that they created. It is an extremely tough situation to try to change a landscape that needed changing decades sooner. Many of these people are on a fixed budget. They can't afford the change to a lower maintenance landscape that is needed and they lack the physical ability to do it themselves. They are trapped and afraid and this is a terrible situation to be in. They are not controlling change; change is controlling them.

Growing fruit-bearing trees can take a few years, so you'll want to plan ahead.

You can avoid being trapped by your landscape by making changes as you move forward to reduce maintenance and inputs to your landscape. Creating an eco-friendly yard is all about building flexibility and change right into your plans. You start out single, add a partner, perhaps add children, some day the children leave, your job changes, but hopefully your partner or spouse doesn't change. Your life is all about change. Creating the systems of change in your landscape will provide constant and continuous rewards for you and others.

Start change today so you can be in control; have it just the way you want it, without hassle, and have fun looking forward to change.

Chapter 14

Where in the World are You?

I was surprised when I traveled to Hawaii some years ago and discovered that there were almost no foods from the islands in local grocery stores, but there were apples from Washington State! There was however, the largest aisle that I have ever seen of Spam® in all sorts of different sizes, flavors and levels of heat. This really shouldn't have been a shock. My local supermarkets rarely have foods from Wisconsin. My old neighbor and friend, Maurice, told me that as a truck driver he often took loads of Wisconsin potatoes to Florida and brought back Florida potatoes to Wisconsin. That's 1,800 miles (2,897km) each way! The reason for this was because of the demand for different varieties for processing, the brokerage of potatoes where a fraction of a cent determines the sale, and transportation was so cheap.

To solve our problem of finding Hawaiian fruits and vegetables, we went to all the farmer's markets that we could find. Even their offerings seemed to be limited to pineapple and local bananas. Maybe it was the time of year. Spotting a nearly ripe breadfruit in the landscape of the condominium we stayed at we picked it and prepared it. It was delicious. People in Hawaii don't typically eat breadfruit, but for hundreds of years at least, it was a staple for natives and visitors.

This book was designed for you to use in the place you live now. Creating a sustainable or eco-friendly yard is all about using the local resources you have where you live. Many of the things I've shown you that I do can be done where you live. You might have different plants, animals, soils and weather, but that doesn't change the basic premise of creating benefits for yourself from your yard. Remember, my interest is not in having you do typical gardening where you spend a lot of time, effort and money trying to create an artificial situation. Rather, inventory the things you have to use and begin using them in a productive way. Many of the things that will benefit us today are rooted in the past.

You still can use a 100-year-old wheelbarrow like this one, and the iron wheel means that you will never have a flat tire.

LEARN FROM YOUR ENVIRONMENT — PAST AND PRESENT

THE SIMPLE LIFE FROM YEARS PAST

Quick, ask someone who is 70, 80 or 90 years old — time is running out. These are not only the smartest people on the planet, but they are also the healthiest. They grew up in a time when modern medicine was rapidly evolving (without all of the pharmaceutical ads on TV) and they had the best diet of any generation in history. Their food was not over-processed and they used locally produced products, crops and energy. My grandparents, uncles and aunts did not use pesticides on their dairy farm or on their cash crops because they couldn't afford them. They were the first organic farmers and this occurred from 1900 to 1980. We can't turn the clock back and live 100 years in the past. We can, however, take that proven science and technology that was refined then and combine the useful things into our modern living situation. Having the internal combustion engine and advanced forms of communications are really minor conveniences compared to the centuries of knowledge that are available for us to use to improve our standard of living through sustainability.

You can build earth-sheltered and solar-heated chicken coops like this one for cold climates. A raised door and perch allows chickens to leave and enter at will without the worry of predators getting in.

THE ADVENT OF CENTRAL HEAT AND AIR CONDITIONING

You might need to look back hundreds of years in the climate where you live. How can these ancient ways of creating comfort apply to how we live now? The masonry heater in our home is the same design used in 1400 A.D. in Europe when they were having their own energy crisis. They were running out of wood for fuel and needed better ways to utilize it.

HOME, BUSINESS AND ANIMAL SHELTERS CONSTRUCTED FOR CLIMATE

In Wisconsin, we had barns (some still exist) where the loft stored hay and the lower level milking parlor was where the cows were milked. The thick walls of the lower level and the hay above created a space where cows and people benefited from a naturally heated and air-conditioned space. These were some of the first earth-sheltered structures in the United States. Modern dairies with large un-insulated pole barns have no protection. If we have an old-fashioned winter where it gets down to -35°F (-37°C) what will happen?

*Yes, homemade doughnuts can be a healthy desert when you chop the wood,
build the fire, make the dough and have a modest serving.*

YOUR ANCESTORS' DIET

A lot of effort has gone into genealogy recently as people try to reconnect to their past. Your genetic background has a lot to do with how past ancestors made their living and what they ate. Your health, diet and fitness are directly related to what you do and how you eat. Raise vegetables, fruits and animals for food that can put you back in touch with your ancestors and give you a healthier lifestyle.

DECAY-RESISTANT TREES

In Wisconsin, we can grow "teak." Yes, we have naturally rot-resistant hardwoods just like the imported teak. They are white oak, black locust and black walnut. These are beautiful woods that grow locally, are low in cost and easily can rival teak in durability and appearance. We also have two varieties of cedar that are naturally resistant to decay. Yet, we regularly import African, South American, and chemically treated Canadian woods for use in decks and other outdoor uses. Naturally rot-resistant woods, grasses (like bamboo), and shrubs provide durable building materials for a variety of uses. Whether you need posts, fencing materials, or building supplies, you probably have locally grown trees and other plants that will provide you with a variety of materials.

We used naturally rot-resistant black locust and black walnut for the floor of our exterior porch 13 years ago and it's still doing fine.

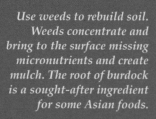

Use weeds to rebuild soil. Weeds concentrate and bring to the surface missing micronutrients and create mulch. The root of burdock is a sought-after ingredient for some Asian foods.

CHANGES IN YOUR SOIL

While visiting Fort McCoy, a military training facility in Wisconsin, I noticed ruts in the soil left by tanks from training during World War II. Over 75 years have past and large trees have grown up between the tracks, but burdock, a common agricultural weed on disturbed soils, was still thriving in the ruts. In many cases, wherever you live, your soil has been damaged and no amount of water or fertilizer will fix it. In Wisconsin, clear cutting of the forest and the following fires in the early 1900s severely damaged the soils. People were able to grow a crop for a few years because of the fertilization effect of the ash from the fires. Then, crop failures occurred just like we now see in the rain forest along the equator. Many of our modern suburbs are now located on some of the best soils in the world. Unfortunately, the soils have been compacted, profiles were changed and also treated with a variety of chemicals and wastes. Regardless of where you live, adding organic material, loosening compacted soil, and creating structures to allow natural rainfall to slowly be absorbed will benefit your soil. Naturally occurring microorganisms will return, nitrogen-fixing plants can be established and desirable vegetation can replace non-beneficial plants.

REUSE, REDUCE AND RECYCLE

Can you use what is being thrown away? In my area, people regularly put out leaves, grass clippings and branches for municipal pick-up. Then, they drive to the city recycling site and haul back wood chips and compost for their garden. There is a tremendous economic and energy cost in doing this. It is better to reuse what you can on your own property. The mantra of many gardening "experts" is don't put meat or cheese in your compost pile because it will attract undesirable animals. My question is, why would you put meat or cheese in your compost pile? Don't you normally eat those things? If they've gone bad, don't you know someone with chickens? Besides, what are you supposed to do with those chipmunks and other rodents that you've been shooting with your pellet gun or shotgun. (In Australia you'll have to use a slingshot or trap since guns are highly regulated.) Adding dead animals to your compost pile is totally acceptable as they are high in nitrogen. Isn't it amazing that people will actually go to the store and purchase bone meal for their garden when they are putting bones in the garbage to be hauled to the landfill? So what if a crow carries off a few! Whatever someone else is throwing out, could be desirable material for some project on your property. If it has lived once, it can live again as a material in your landscape.

Build a walkway to take you to places in your landscape.

HEALTH BENEFITS FROM YOUR YARD

You eat healthier, exercise better, relax easier, have more control and you can create more fun nights on your own property. Is it any wonder that many remedies stress that they're made from naturally occurring substances? If you don't have an outside area at your home to enjoy and where you can relax in nature, then you are neglecting your health. Improve your health by simply spending more time outside doing whatever you like, as long as you limit the use of power equipment and pesticides.

PLAY IN YOUR YARD

Of any society, we seem to have some of the most sought-after recreational opportunities ever imagined. Most of them are not healthy. Swimming in a chemically treated pool is not good for your skin, eyes or lungs. Golfing on a course treated daily with pesticides may lead to health problems. Soccer on a fertilized, irrigated, and yes, pesticide-treated field is not a safe place for children of any age. Driving to the gym and working out in a heated and air-conditioned space might be convenient, but it does not have the same health advantages as being outside. It creates pollution and waste instead of being a creative activity. Let's have the gym activity, like riding a stationary bike, at least power the laundromat next door. It is ludicrous that we air condition gyms so people can "work out" in comfort.

> *Being unhealthy may be caused by your immediate environment and it also causes problems for the environment. Almost all pharmaceutical drugs are now found in surface and ground water. Yes, that is probably the water you are drinking. Those same drugs are showing up in fish and other animals. The pollution created by drugs is not just because people are flushing unused medications down the toilet, but because medications are not used up by your body and are eliminated from your body with other wastes.*

A bench placed in a shady spot is great for reading or decompressing after work.

A romantic spot might be good for your health!

Place old bottles on end and set in a copper bowl to create a unique fire pit for after-dark enjoyment around the fire.

Build an easy-to-use outdoor sink and faucet that makes hand washing more like play.

The current definition of "play" usually refers to highly organized, fossil-fuel wasting, parent-pushing, doting coaches, inner-focused, costly, environmentally damaging, lack of any cognitive skills, win at any cost, be a super-star, aggression oriented with no long-term value activities. Even employers are taking a second look at the standard of "hire an athlete" to get a good team player because team sports are no longer about the team. What does this have to do with your eco-friendly yard? Everything! Your yard should be a fun place for kids, adults, and yes, even pets, to discover, enjoy, learn and grow. Excluding nature from your yard reduces the quality of play. Most yards with a mowed lawn and a few boring shrubs are simply a garbage dump (notice I didn't say desert — deserts can be quite vital) for intellectual, healthy play. Playing in your yard can be enriching, revitalizing, offer teaching moments and it can turn play into an activity that provides lifelong experiences. Play can have a positive impact for the players and the environment, but only if your yard has diversity with nature designed into it.

Eliminate soil tilling entirely or limit it to small areas for specific crops.

Garlic bulbs (center) can be grown in two seasons from the seed head bulblets (left) if you don't have enough cloves that take a season to mature (right).

HOW DOES YOUR GARDEN GROW?

I receive evaluations from seminars I present where a small percentage of participants who are gardeners actually are offended and confused by what I teach regarding sustainable landscapes. Gardening has devolved in the United States to a meaningless hobby for the most part. People spend a lot more effort on the details and getting it right in model railroading than they do in gardening. While people are doing more things outside in their yard, they are doing less gardening. Most people don't want an activity where they don't see a reward and many people are not seeing a reward for all that hard work. As a result, I don't teach gardening as it is currently practiced, and I advocate against using the term in most situations. Most standard gardening practices include difficult composting methods, using lots of pesticides, labor-intensive work for the hands and knees, frivolous tools, unneeded tilling of soil, irrigation dependency, deficiency in applied science, poor planning, focus on annual plants, just the right clothes, too many seed catalogs and an over concern about weeds, insects and diseases that are just plain wrong. University extension services and rapidly diminishing gardening clubs are left wondering why more people aren't interested in gardening. Your eco-friendly

yard does not have to include any of these practices. This frees you to concentrate on what is truly important to you, not what has been published in the tens of thousands of gardening books from the last few decades that mostly recycle the same content from fifty yeas ago. Be prepared when you start projects in your eco-friendly yard. You will be the talk of your gardening neighbors. I am always surprised at the number of things that I've accomplished successfully for years for myself and my customers that some gardeners still say, "It can't be done," "I've never seen that before," "It'll never work" or "I didn't know that could be done." I'm not dreaming up this stuff. Everything I do has been done by someone before me. As a society, we've forgotten, and are now rediscovering, the new old ways of doing sustainable things.

To find your place in the world, start asking questions. You can create your own eco-friendly yard rapidly. Answering the questions before you start may be time-consuming but necessary. You can find the answers for where you live, but you might have to do some deep digging and some careful observing. You can do it!

Chapter 15
Safety

YOUR UNIQUE SITUATION

In a few hours one November afternoon, I installed, planted and fenced an entire no-till vegetable garden for my friends and customers, Miguel and Pramela. Miguel assisted me, which helped him understand the plants and how to maintain the space. Almost no one in our northern climate plants a garden in November. Yet, this can be the best time of the year to establish a sustainable garden space that will take very little effort to maintain and provide homegrown foods indefinitely without replanting.

There are four general areas where you will want to understand your unique situation. Understanding your situation is pivotal to get the results you desire and to create a safe environment.

YOU WILL BE DOING THINGS

Perhaps planting a garden in the opposite season of everyone else is different than what is currently practiced in your area. One action creates another action. Do you know what that will be? Researching weather, wildlife, levels of precipitation, understanding domestic and wild plants and animals, knowledge of fire dangers, and knowing who and when someone will use the property that you are changing, are just some of the important details you'll want to know and use.

YOUR CLIMATE AND GEOGRAPHIC AREA

To complicate the situation even more, it is very likely that there will be great variability within a few miles, or even a few hundred feet, from where you live. Where I live, we have frost pockets, areas where cold air pools usually at night. These areas can have a killing frost even in the middle of summer. This would be a bad area to grow many garden crops but it excels for growing cranberries. In mountainous areas, changes in elevation over a small area can make a huge difference in what will grow and what won't. Your climate may be prone to flash floods, dust storms, poisonous animals, toxic plants or months without rain. All of these things can affect soils, structures and your personal health. You will derive a greater level of enjoyment and security in your eco-friendly yard when you have a deep understanding of your climate and geography. If you work in cooperation with your climate and geography, you can create a great place to live and play.

Two laying hens will produce eight to 12 eggs a week and eat food scraps. (But this won't be happening in my city.)

YOUR CULTURE OR THE CULTURES OF THOSE AROUND YOU

The world view may be that the only active culture where I live is found in yogurt, but I would disagree. A city near me recently went through the process of becoming an eco-municipality. I suggested that residents be allowed to have two or three laying hens. They are great at consuming food waste and turning it into eggs, producing a high-quality fertilizer, don't make much noise, unlike roosters, and can be kept in a small space. I was informed that this idea was removed from the final plan because of a concern someone had about a neighbor from a different culture in relationship to how they might begin using their property. This is a city where you could have, up to this point, any number of dogs or cats on your property without special permission. What does this tell you about this particular culture? It has gone to the dogs!

Peer pressure and laws will make a difference. Sometimes, it doesn't pay to ask because many people won't even know what you are talking about. Do some basic investigation so you won't break any laws and talk to your immediate neighbors about it. When the neighbors see the benefit to them, like farm-fresh eggs, they are likely to be a lot more supportive of what you do. Start out small and experiment. It's a great way to test things and stay under the radar until you can show positive results that don't hurt you or bother the neighbors.

SENSITIVE ENVIRONMENTS

All environments are sensitive, but some are affected more quickly and can be permanently damaged by just a few hours of mucking around. Our glacier-formed lakes can be easily polluted and our highly erosive soils in our "central sands" area are examples of sensitive environments that are degraded rapidly by human activities. Most of our lakes have no exits, so what gets put in the lake stays in the lake. When our wide expanses of sand plains are plowed, wind easily can move tons of soil and the applied fertilizer and pesticides dozens of miles in an instant.

When I see another resort with flush toilets and irrigated lawn being built on a coral island, I am deeply disturbed, even though I may never visit. This type of environment has only a shallow lens of fresh water below the surface. Pumping fresh water out of the ground faster than it is replenished by rain results in salty sea water invading and taking its place and the island begins to die. In this situation, the only water that should be used is the rain that comes off roofs and is stored for domestic uses. Using plants and planting methods that don't need irrigation are critical to preserving all life on these islands.

Research areas where you live to find out if your environment is sensitive to certain things. Your actions can have a positive effect that won't damage your property, keeps your neighbor's property safe and safeguards the entire environment.

TOOL AND EQUIPMENT SAFETY

Initially, tools and equipment are needed to create your eco-friendly yard. I support the reasonable use of these things because, when done right, you end up reducing the long-term need for fossil-fuel powered tools.

You can get hurt in a variety of ways while engaged in landscape activities — I speak from experience. I'm working on different properties daily, with different challenges, and doing different things. For me to continue to do what I enjoy; I chose not to hurt myself. That's right! When someone gets hurt, they chose to do it in almost all situations. There are safe ways to do things and you need to learn how to implement them. What's the best way to learn about safety? From other people's experiences, not your own, because it hurts too much.

Before using any hand tool, power tool, piece of equipment or applying chemicals, READ THE DIRECTIONS! Use the owner's manual or go online to the manufacturer's site to find information. I haven't purchased a power tool yet that didn't come with a complete set of directions and safety tips. If you rent tools, ask the rental place to allow you to read the directions, or have someone show you how, before you take the tool. The Internet has made finding directions from manufacturers very easy.

When working with power tools, put the children and pets away. Children don't belong around equipment that can hurt them. You can be easily distracted, which could result in an injury to yourself.

One of the most common tools for injuries in the yard is the lawn mower. When you properly design the size and layout of your lawn to gain more benefits from your eco-friendly yard, you also reduce the chance of a lawn mower injury. Adults and children are regularly injured by lawn mowers. I have seen toddlers riding on the mower deck, just inches from the spinning blade of riding lawn mowers with a smiling mom driving. This is plain and simple child abuse no matter how much fun the child has or how cute the parent thinks it is. If the child isn't injured immediately, there still will be hearing loss and health issues related to exhaust emissions from these mowers.

Cutting up wood with a sharp chain saw can be fun and empowering, but chain saws have their problems. Chain saws are a rising star in the injury category. Even the smallest chain saws have about 30 inches (76cm) of totally exposed, unguarded, cutting surface. There are a few other power tools made that don't have guards for protection and bring users into close proximity to the business end of the tool. With the advent of inexpensive chain saws sold at the discount stores, it is no wonder that injuries are increasing for homeowners using this tool while at the same time injuries to professionals seem to be declining. How can this be?

Professional chain saw users have embraced safety equipment, instruction and proper maintenance over the past decade — home users have not. I had an emergency room physician visiting who owned and used a chain saw but didn't have the safety equipment and he didn't seem concerned. Perhaps he has access to better medical services than the rest of us. Every chain saw user should have a pair of chaps to protect the legs, a helmet with screen to protect the head and eyes, and hearing protection. A class in proper use and care of chain saws should also be mandatory for anyone who uses one. Combining a chain saw, an extension ladder and a tree can be a deadly, or, at least, a lifetime-crippling activity. If you know someone doing this, please advise them that I will help them update their will — there's a really good chance I could be an heir. Professional tree workers don't mix extension ladders and chain saws and neither should you!

CALL BEFORE YOU DIG

Perhaps you have heard the familiar slogan "call before you dig." Have your utility company mark specific areas before digging on your property and always follow their instructions for digging. Many places have a service where utilities identify lines and pipes they own. Keep in mind, privately installed electric and gas lines may require you to hire an electrician or plumber to locate these. You will want to plan ahead for this because it may take several days to have the lines marked. You could assume a huge liability when you cause damage to utilities. Not only are you responsible for the repair, but you may also be responsible for any losses to others. A few years ago, I had a potential customer call me after he and a buddy on a "weekend warrior" project using a bulldozer struck a buried electric cable. He only cut off the power to his house, but the resulting short destroyed most of the appliances and electronics in his neighbor's house. Many people do not have enough home insurance to cover the type of damage that can occur from damaging public utilities.

PLANT SAFETY

Most plants will never hurt you, and I think too much time is spent scaring people about perceived threats from plants. With that said, it is easy to stay safe around even the most dangerous plants in the world by using these two simple rules. You learned this as a toddler; No. 1. Do not put anything in your mouth that you are not familiar with. No. 2. Do not remove your clothes and roll around in any strange plants. Not eating and not touching plants or their fruit is common sense. Not touching unknown plants includes not coming in contact with juice, sawdust, fruits, leaves and even root systems.

One other common sense rule — don't inhale. Yes, just like a former president once said. Inhaling smoke from burning plants, trees, shrubs or herbs can cause immediate damage, as in the case of smoke from poison ivy or long-term lung damage from wood smoke. If you have an eco-friendly yard, except for cooking fires, you won't be burning unknown debris anyway. So as long as you avoid fire-fighting duty, you should be fine.

Picking wild plants requires a level of understanding and education. I had dinner with a friend that explained she won't eat wild mushrooms because a couple she knew were wild mushroom experts. The experts died when they made an error in identification and consumed a highly toxic mushroom. Many wild mushroom hunters in my area only pick one or two kinds of easily identifiable mushrooms. Portage County has a large number of Polish people who hunt *grzyby* (pronounced locally - "jeeba"). Most only pick the button mushroom and picking is an experience involving three generations. Children, parents and grandparents all participate. In this way, decades of experience is used to identify and pick mushrooms. This is a good practice and results in a high level of safety for the pickers and the eaters.

I know that plants in this book are safe to use and eat as shown to the best of my knowledge, but you should always identify plants prior to use with a plant guide and personal assistance from those who have experience in your climate. Start out using common plants on your own property that are easy to identify and not easily confused with other plants. Learn safely as you acquire more plants that are familiar to you.

LAWS, REGULATIONS AND PERMITS

Landscaping activities are coming under increased scrutiny by regulators. Recently, the building code for Wisconsin added soil slope requirements around homes. You would think that sloping soil away from homes in a climate where most homes have basements would be common sense. However, this addition to the building code was implemented because of the many instances of wet or flooded basements caused by improper grading around homes.

Contact your local zoning and planning department to find out what ordinances might affect your yard project. When landscaping, you may need approval from state, federal and local government agencies. You may be able to create your own plan. If not, get help with a drawn plan and specification list that would make permitting easier. As the property owner, you are responsible for acquiring all government approval and confirmation of compliance with regulations and restrictions for your plan prior to commencing any construction. Your goal in producing a sustainable landscape should be to do the project once. Failing to follow laws in this regard could cause you to redo your landscape and may result in fines for breaking the law.

Activities, projects and methods I show in this book are safe and legal for me to do where I live. You need to check before you start a project to see if any changes are required where you live.

SURVEYS

You wouldn't want to build a fence on the neighbor's property or cut down his trees, would you? While using an adjoining property can be a great way to add to your eco-friendly yard, it's probably not a good idea to do that without permission. Use land surveys and surveyors to make sure that your hard work is being done on your own property.

I receive calls every year regarding trees being removed by trespassers. In almost all cases, it was just an error in identifying the property line. This seems like a small problem until you realize that laws protecting property are quite strong in many states. Trees are not valued by just their replacement cost. They are valued based on all of the values that they bring to the property. For example, a 12-inch (30cm)-diameter oak tree that is strategically located might be worth thousands of dollars, not the several hundred to replace it with one from the nursery. In Wisconsin, when you start a fire, you are liable up to double the damages if it travels beyond your property lines and creates damage.

Surveys are a low-cost way to identify property lines. Surveyors can find existing property lines or add additional lines, as is the case with subdividing property. Once the corners of your property are clear, it is easy for you to run a bit of twine between markers to lay out the entire property. Don't trust someone's past knowledge about your property lines. If you cannot find the original corners of your property, usually marked by a buried iron stake or concrete monument, then it is time to hire a surveyor.

As you can see, there are quite a few areas in safety. It's not just about avoiding cuts and scratches. Insurance costs, medical costs, lost time, inconvenience, equipment damage, fires and the personal toll these things take can turn a landscape into a horror. It doesn't have to be this way. Choose to have a well-planned, safe and enjoyable experience with your eco-friendly yard by following the easy safety recommendations stated in this chapter.

Zone Map

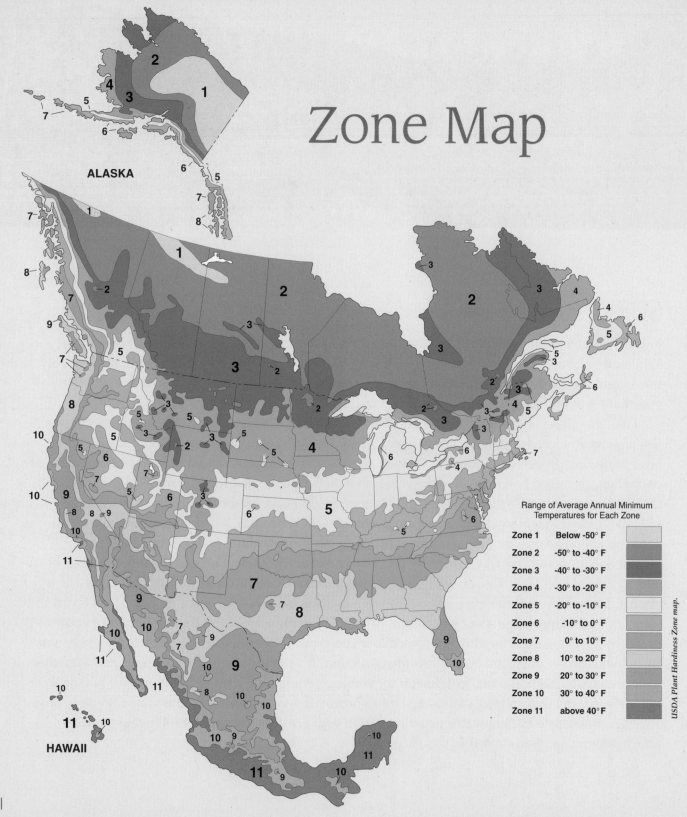

ALASKA

HAWAII

Range of Average Annual Minimum
Temperatures for Each Zone

Zone 1	Below -50° F	
Zone 2	-50° to -40° F	
Zone 3	-40° to -30° F	
Zone 4	-30° to -20° F	
Zone 5	-20° to -10° F	
Zone 6	-10° to 0° F	
Zone 7	0° to 10° F	
Zone 8	10° to 20° F	
Zone 9	20° to 30° F	
Zone 10	30° to 40° F	
Zone 11	above 40° F	

USDA Plant Hardiness Zone map.

Metric Table

LENGTH

IMPERIAL UNIT	METRIC UNIT
Inch	25.40 millimeters
Inch	2.54 centimeters
Foot	30.48 centimeters
Yard	0.91 meters
Mile	1.61 kilometers

METRIC UNIT	IMPERIAL UNIT
Millimeter	0.039 inches
Centimeter	0.39 inches
Meter	3.28 feet
Meter	1.09 yards
Kilometer	0.62 miles

WEIGHT (OR MASS)

IMPERIAL UNIT	METRIC UNIT
Ounce	28.35 grams
Pound	0.45 kilograms
UK ton (2240 pounds)	1.02 metric tons
US ton (2000 pounds)	0.91 tons

METRIC UNIT	IMPERIAL UNIT
Gram	0.035 ounces
Kilogram	2.21 pounds
Metric ton (1000kg)	0.98 UK tons
Metric ton(1000kg)	1.10 US tons

TEMPERATURE

FAHRENHEIT

°F = (°C x 1.8) + 32

For example: (20°C x 1.8) + 32 = (36) + 32 = 68°F

CELSIUS

°C = (°F - 32) ÷ 1.8

For example: (68°F - 32) ÷ 1.8 = (36) ÷ 1.8 = 20°C

PRESSURE

IMPEIAL UNIT	METRIC UNIT
1 pound per square inch (psi)	6894.76 pascal (Pa=N/m²)
1 pound per square inch (psi)	6.90 kilopascal (kN/m²)
1 pound per square inch (psi)	0.69 bar

METRIC UNIT	IMPERIAL UNIT
10,000 Pascal (Pa=N/m²)	1.45 pound per square inch (psi)
10 Kilopascal (kN/m²)	1.45 pound per square inch (psi)
0.1 Bar	1.45 pound per square inch (psi)

VOLUME

IMPERIAL UNIT	METRIC UNIT
Teaspoon (UK)	5.92 milliliters
Teaspoon (US)	4.93 milliliters
Tablespoon (UK)	17.76 milliliters
Tablespoon (US)	14.79 milliliters
Fluid ounce (UK)	28.41 milliliters
Fluid ounce (US)	29.57 milliliters
Pint (UK)	0.57 liters
Pint (US)	0.47 liters
Quart (UK)	1.14 liters
Quart (US)	0.95 liters
Gallon (UK)	4.55 liters
Gallon (US)	3.79 liters

METRIC UNIT	IMPERIAL UNIT
Milliliter	0.17 teaspoons (UK)
Milliliter	0.20 teaspoons (US)
10 Milliliter	0.56 tablespoons (UK)
10 Milliliter	0.68 tablespoons (US)
100 Milliliter	3.52 fluid ounces (UK)
100 Milliliter	3.38 fluid ounces
Liter	1.76 pints (UK)
Liter	2.11 pints (US)
Liter	0.88 quarts (UK)
Liter	1.06 quarts (US)
Liter	0.22 gallon (UK)
Liter	0.26 gallon (US)

AREA

IMPERIAL UNIT	METRIC UNIT
Square inch	6.45 square centimeters
Square foot	0.09 square meters
Square yard	0.84 square meters
Square mile	2.60 square kilometers
Cubic foot	0.028 cubic meters
Cubic yard	0.76 cubic meters
Acre	0.40 hectare

METRIC UNIT	IMPERIAL UNIT
Square centimeter	0.16 square inches
Square meter	1.20 square yard
Square kilometer	0.39 square miles
Cubic meter	35.23 cubic feet
Cubic meter	1.35 cubic yards
Hectare	2.47 acres

Glossary

Black locust: (Robinia pseudoacacia) Deciduous tree in the legume family. Rot-resistant and extremely hard wood is very abrasive to cutting tools.

Black walnut: (Juglans nigra) High-quality rot-resistant wood of medium density is prized for furniture making. Trees with defects or knots have little value, but are great for outdoor construction.

Brick oven: The middle-ages answer to the microwave. A very efficient structure used for cooking with wood. Generally constructed as a dome of fireproof masonry where a fire is built inside the oven. Food is cooked through radiant heat stored in the oven floor and walls.

Brush saw: Gas-powered saw with a revolving circular blade used for cutting small diameter trees, shrubs and brush.

Brush mower: Used for cutting down plants grown as a mulch material or for cleaning up the garden.

Bungee cords: Heavy, rubber straps with "S" hooks on each end. Used for a variety of purposes to hold things in place.

Burdock: (Arctium lappa) Vigorous biennial with tap roots that can be harvested during the first year. In Japan, it is called *gobo*, in Korea it is called *ueong*, in Italy, Brazil and Portugal, it is known as *bardana*.

Chaps: Leg protectors made with special layers of material designed to stop a chain saw and avoid a trip to the hospital emergency room.

Chop-and-drop: Method of pruning down shrubs and leaving the cuttings to form a layer of mulch.

Cistern: A tank to store rainwater

Compost bin: A place to put yard and kitchen wastes so they will never see the light of day again.

Composting: Dreamed up by gardeners with too much time on their hands. Bacterial action speeds up decomposition of organic wastes, but is left to sit for years because it takes too much work to move around. See compost bin above.

Cord: A unit of cut wood that is 4 feet by 4 feet by 8 feet usually used to describe firewood. Approximately 5 cubic meters.

Corn gluten: Byproduct of the corn (Zea Mays L.) wet-milling process, corn gluten meal is a natural pre-emergent herbicide.

Cranberry bogs: Below-grade fields that are flooded for frost protection and harvest of cranberries (Vaccinium macrocarpon).

Drip irrigation: Method of applying drops of water to the base or root system of a plant.

Eco-municipality: A mostly feel-good attempt recently by cities to make them more livable and promote what a great place it is to live. Most of the possible true benefits of this effort went down the "black hole" known as committees.

Emitters: Devices attached to drip irrigation line to meter out the drop of water.

EPA: United States Environmental Protection Agency. The section of government that gets to decide which poisons they are actually going to license for use, while others in the same agency are responsible to protect us from all of the really bad stuff they are approving.

Female garden hose end: The fitting on the garden hose that has female threads.

Female garden hose threads: Coarse threads on the inside of the fitting designed to be attached to (you guessed it!) male threads on the male garden hose end.

Firebrick: Bricks made from a mixture of clays with varying resistance to heat. Used in brick ovens and masonry heaters.

Gardening: A method employed by wealthy aristocrats and royalty in the past to keep peasants busy on their estates providing just enough income to avoid riots. Now practiced by an aging group of hobbyists and supported by university extensions and the pesticide industry. A labor-intensive method of landscaping, usually creates environmental damage with no redeeming benefits.

Global warming: A potential crisis created by burning fossil fuels. (Everyone else hopes that someone else will do something about it.)

Gray water: Used water from sinks, showers and laundry that can be used for irrigation.

Green: A color - only a color. No longer relevant when used to describe an environmentally friendly product or service because everyone is using this word for everything.

Habitat: All the parts of the environment used by an organism for food, shelter, breeding and recreation (in the case of people).

Hedge trimmers: Large manual scissors or hand-held powered sickle for trimming shrubs.

Hops: (Humulus lupulus) That's kind of fun to say. An aggressive herbaceous perennial vine. Female flower cones are used for flavoring and preserving beer.

Landscape architect: A degreed and licensed landscape planner who is having his "lunch eaten" by engineers and landscape designers. Prone to using computer-aided design, incorporating lots of non-plant material and publishing weird stuff in landscape architecture magazines.

Landscape designer: A term that can be used by anyone and usually is. A person who creates landscape plans without any qualifications. Some are very good and talented, but difficult to find one that understands sustainable concepts.

Landscaper: Anyone with a pick-up truck and a shovel. Often found complaining that they have no work because the home builder does his job now. How hard is it to put a gravel border around a house with few boring shrubs in it? Plows snow in cold climates.

Laying hens: Mature fowl kept for egg production.

LEDs: Light-emitting diodes that are very energy efficient. Found in traffic lights, toys and flashlights. Just starting to be seen in home and landscape use.

Lifestyle: How a person lives or how they want to live.

Male garden hose end: Attaches to the female garden hose end. Has coarse threads on the outside of the fitting. Not to be confused with standard pipe thread.

Masonry heater: Very efficient fireplace technology that uses a long smoke path to store and re-radiate heat from a wood fire.

Micro-irrigation: Low water use irrigation for targeted water application using small sprinklers.

Mini-skid steer: Small, powered machines with wheels or tracks that you stand on or walk behind to operate. Used for moving soil, augering holes, moving pallets and many other uses. Is replacing the shovel, wheelbarrow and large landscape crews because of the simplicity and efficiency of the machine.

Mizzle Wizard: One type of small sprinkler heads used for micro-irrigation.

Mulching lawn mower: Powered lawn mower with a special blade and design for cutting up grass and other light plants into little bits.

Mullein: (Verbascum thapsus and 250 other species) Biennial plant known for its soft fuzzy leaves and its erect flower stalk the second year.

Narrative: A written description of a landscape plan.

Nitrogen-fixing: Describes the process of getting free fertilizer in your landscape. Nitrogen-fixing plants gather nitrogen from the air (which is 80 percent nitrogen) and make it biologically available to other plants.

No-till gardens: An efficient way of raising food crops without cultivating or turning over the soil.

Organic: Supposedly, the classification of a food or fiber crop grown with only safe natural inputs. Since when is natural safe — think of lead, asbestos, mercury, earthquakes and typhoons? Organic products are often treated with natural-occurring pesticides that are non-selective and more environmentally damaging than man-made chemicals. Often, treatment of labor and soil stewardship is not part of organic definitions.

Organic fertilizer: A classification of plant nutrients made from a variety of plants and organisms. Often uses more fossil fuels in growing, production and shipping than the same amount of petroleum-based fertilizers.

Passive solar: Heating with the sun using natural convection instead of fans or pumps.

Peel: A flat piece of wood or metal with a handle used primarily for moving breads into and out of ovens.

Perennial onion: Also called Egyptian, walking onion or multiplier. Can stay in the ground year-round in climates as cold as Zone 3.

Permaculture: Permanent agriculture or permanent culture. Many definitions and not widely known. A growing group of experts are assisting people in meeting their needs on their own properties using efficient methods of land management and specialized cropping systems.

Personality: The feelings that you have within that are expressed in how you do things.

Poison ivy: (Rhus radicans or Toxicondendron radicans) A perennial plant, shrub or vine in the cashew family. All plant parts contain an oil that can cause painful skin blisters through contact of the plant or contact of the oil that has been transferred. The oil can also be carried by smoke from fires and inhaled, damaging the lungs.

Purslane: (Portulaca oleracea) Prostrate, thick, fleshy-stemmed, common garden weed with wedge-shaped leaves. Contains more omega-3 fatty acids than any other known leafy, green plant. Excellent eaten raw as coleslaw, used as a thickener in soups, and fine-roasted with seasonings and olive oil.

Puttering: Time-wasting activities endemic to gardeners.

Rain barrel: Originally, an old wood barrel left at the eaves of a building to collect rainwater in order to avoid the work of carrying or pumping water for drinking, washing and cooking. In modern times, a purchased plastic drum for homeowners to practice ineffective forms of garden irrigation and water conservation.

Rain garden: Usually, a small depression in the yard created by gardeners because they were told this is a good thing for the environment. Turns into a weedy hole or a mosquito breeding puddle and becomes another neglected part of the property.

Retaining wall: Construction project for grown men who want something bigger than Legos™. Usually contrived structures that some people use to make their home look more like a castle. Unneeded wall for holding back soil when proper grading would have worked better.

Sickle mower: Powered mower with a reciprocating blade for cutting grasses to be used for hay and straw mulch.

Solarize: A method of using a sheet of plastic over the ground to heat the soil. Incorrectly thought of as a way to kill weed seeds.

Solar panels: Structures designed to turn sunlight into energy. Can be photo-voltaic (electrical producing), hot water or hot-air panels.

Sprinklers: Generally refers to wasteful lawn irrigation devices for spraying water, some of which actually goes on the grass.

Stargazing: Looking at the stars. An activity that is getting harder to do because of light pollution.

Sunchokes: (Helianthus tuberosus) A variety of perennial sunflower grown for its edible tuber. Sometimes called Jerusalem artichoke. It is neither from Jerusalem nor is it an artichoke. Some gardeners freak out because of the pernicious nature of this plant. Mowing it or eating it is the best way to get rid of it if you don't want it.

Survey: A process of finding and marking property lines. Managed by those licensed or certified as surveyors.

Sustainable: A true benefit for you, others and the environment. In many situations, an over-used word with whole books being written to define it.

Swale: Shallow-dug linear depression. Can be level, on-grade or off-grade. Used to move, hold, distribute and absorb water to create multiple benefits. Can incorporate desirable vegetation and crops.

Synthetic weed barrier: A plastic, woven or non-woven fabric purchased by gardeners and landscapers in the mistaken belief that this will somehow stop weeds from growing. Becomes intertwined with desirable plant root systems damaging the plant and making the barrier difficult to remove.

Tenon: Half of a wood joint that can be a round, square or rectangular projection that fits into a matching size and shape hole called a mortise.

Thermal inversion: A weather condition where cool air is held close to the earth's surface by warm air hovering over it. Can occur on clear nights, in valleys and along ocean shorelines, and prevents smog and smoke from rising and dispersing, creating localized air pollution.

Weed whips: Also called string trimmers, weed whackers and from my Australian friends, whipper-snippers. A powered trimmer with a spinning disk holding flexible filament for cutting grasses and weeds and girdling desirable trees, if you are not careful.

Wild rice: (Genus zizania) Group of grasses with edible seeds that grows in shallow water. A total of four species native to North America and Asia. Now grown as a cultivated crop in various areas of the world and viewed as an invasive species in New Zealand.

White oak: (Quercus alba) Rot-resistant hardwood tree with edible acorns. Closed cellular structure called tyloses prevents water movement in the wood, making white oak ideal for wine barrels.

Resources and Supplies

Creating an eco-friendly yard and a sustainable landscape has never been easier. This is a great time in history because you have a whole world of information available to you through the Internet. As much as I don't really care for computers; companies selling products, services and supplies have found that using the Internet as their sales catalog can reach more people and do so effectively. For sustainable products and services, the Internet will be the way for you to find help rapidly at this critical time. I've provided just a sampling of resources so that you can get your feet wet in finding sustainable resources on the Internet and in turn can make good purchasing decisions.

BRICK OVENS

Italian made: Forno Brava
www.fornobravo.com

French made: Fayol
www.lepanyol.com

CAST-IRON COOKWARE

Special Note: Due to worldwide concern regarding health, safety, and quality of foods and products that come in contact with food; when purchasing cast-iron cookware, patronize manufacturers in countries where you can verify reputation of the manufacturer and that their product is tested for safety. There are lots of cheap cast-iron cookware products available that may not have the quality or integrity that you need. Do not purchase cast-iron cookware that has a synthetic "nonstick" coating because it will burn and chip off and you will eat it. Fired, enamel coatings that do not contain lead are fine for some uses. I've listed the manufacturer I know, but there should be one or more in the country you live in.

U.S.: Lodge Manufacturing Company *(only U.S. manufacturer)*
www.lodgemfg.com

DRIP IRRIGATION

U.S. and International: DIG Corporation
www.digcorp.com

U.K., Ireland and Northern Europe: Revaho U.K.
www.revaho-landscape.co.uk

MASONRY HEATERS

Information: Wood Heat Organization, Inc.
www.woodheat.org

North America, Europe and Japan: The Masonry Heater Association
www.mha-net.org

Canada and U.S.: Temp-Cast Enviroheat, Ltd.
www.tempcast.com

North America, Europe and Russia: Tulikivi
www.tulikivi.com

Wisconsin: Gimme Shelter Construction
www.gimmeshelteronline.com

SOLAR SYSTEMS

Backwoods Solar Electric Systems
www.backwoodssolar.com

Unirac, Inc.
www.unirac.com

U.S.: Lake Michigan Wind and Sun, LTD
www.windandsun.com

U.K.: Wind and Sun, LTD
www.windandsun.co.uk

TENON-MAKING TOOL

Lumberjack Tools
www.lumberjacktools.com

LANDSCAPE POWER EQUIPMENT

Sweden and worldwide: Husqvarna® AB
www.husqvarna.com

Germany and worldwide: Stihl®, Inc.
www.stihl.com

Canada and U.S.: Ramrod Equipment
www.ramrodequip.com

TO CONTACT TOM GIROLAMO:

Eco-Building & Forestry, LLC.
1058 DuBay Dr. • Mosinee, WI 54455
Email: tom@landscapes4life.com
Phone: 715-344-2817
www.landscapes4life.com

Index

advanced entertainment areas, 85

algae, 50, 201-202

algaecides, 201-202

aquatic plants, 197-198, 201

arborist, 97, 163, 255

asparagus, 20, 125, 210

batteries, 70, 73

battery, 65, 67, 69-71, 73, 75, 77, 95

benefits, 11, 15, 17, 25-27, 29-30, 33, 55-57, 59, 95, 123, 127, 147, 152, 178-179, 183, 189-190, 192, 196-198, 204-205, 207-210, 213-214, 219, 227, 240, 248, 250

bistro chairs, 113, 117

bistro table, 107, 113

black plastic, 155-156

blowing out irrigation lines, 138

bold personality, 63, 65, 95-96

brick oven, 31, 39, 56, 60, 86-89, 91, 248, 251

brush mowers, 53, 248

brush saws, 51, 175-176, 248

budget, 43-44, 63, 85, 217

budgeting, 43-44

bungee cord, 105

call before you dig, 241

chickens, 26, 56, 59-60, 64-66, 69, 152, 204, 212, 221, 225

chipper, 53, 163

chop-and-drop, 149, 170, 175, 179, 181, 248

cisterns, 60, 134

clay, 88, 135, 197, 201

climate, 13, 17, 27, 35, 37, 59, 86, 88, 97, 124, 129, 138, 156, 170, 173, 180, 187, 190, 193, 204, 207, 209-210, 221, 235, 242-243, 249

compost bin, 19, 248

compost pile, 19, 153, 225

composting, 19, 153, 157, 232, 248

compressor, 138-139

cork end table, 115, 117, 141

corn gluten, 127, 248

culture, 188, 236, 250

decision makers, 43

decomposition, 152-153, 155, 163, 165, 248

design analysis, 45

design, 2, 29, 33, 41-42, 45, 47, 49, 60, 88, 97, 171, 197, 202, 221, 240, 249, 255

diet, 134, 220, 222

drip irrigation line, 129-131, 133, 136, 248

drip irrigation, 60, 128-131, 133-134, 136, 147, 151, 183, 189, 248, 251

earth-sheltered, 221

easy-going personality, 151-152, 178, 180

ecosystem, 201

Eco-Weed Barrier, 159

efficiency, 25-27, 29-30, 59, 136, 249

energy, 11, 18, 20-21, 27, 33, 41, 59-60, 63, 97, 125, 149, 190-193, 195, 220-221, 225, 249-250

environment, 15, 27, 33, 56, 127, 135, 149, 181, 185, 189, 202, 210, 220, 227, 231, 235, 237, 249-250

equipment, 5, 49, 53, 70, 138, 179, 187, 197, 213, 227, 239-240, 245, 251, 255

erosion, 18, 79, 152, 179, 191, 193-194, 197-198, 209

fencer, 64

fences, 65-67, 95, 103, 105, 151, 195, 245

fertilizer, 21, 26, 43, 51, 157, 192, 208, 212-213, 224, 236-237, 249

fossil fuels, 181, 248-249

fun personality, 99, 101, 123-124

gardening, 20, 23, 49-50, 156, 165, 183, 219, 225, 232-233, 248

geographic area, 235

gray water, 101-103, 248

ground cover plants, 51, 173, 180-181

groundwater, 188, 192, 204

habitat, 33, 60, 201-202, 249

health, 29, 53, 55, 57, 134, 208, 222, 227, 229, 235, 240, 251

hedge trimmers, 51, 174-175, 249

hedge, 51, 149, 174-175, 249

hydrologist, 197

integrating structures, 37

irrigation, 33, 60, 73, 79-81, 83, 128-131, 133-136, 138-139, 147, 151, 183, 187, 189, 192, 197-198, 204, 209, 232, 237, 248-251

kachelofen, 207

kangs, 207

laws, 237, 243, 245

lifestyle pyramid, 5, 58-60

lifestyle, 5, 11, 15, 17, 21, 23, 25, 28-30, 49, 55-61, 96, 127, 151, 189, 207, 210, 215, 222, 249, 255

lighting, 5, 37, 69, 73, 77, 95, 99, 202

low-maintenance, 29, 59-60, 189

low-voltage, 77, 95, 202

masonry heater, 60, 207-208, 221, 248-249, 251

micro-irrigation, 79, 134-136, 138-139, 183, 249

micronutrients, 224

microorganisms, 224

mini-skid steers, 53

Mizzle Wizard, 79, 81-83, 134, 249

mulch, 19, 25, 30, 51, 53, 60, 83, 127, 149, 152-153, 155-157, 159-161, 163, 165-171, 174, 176-177, 179-181, 185, 198, 202, 209, 211, 224, 248, 250

mulching lawn mower, 51, 249

municipal water, 134, 209

native plants, 23
natural resources, 5, 60, 255
no-till, 20, 53, 235, 249
nutrients, 51, 127, 179, 187-188, 201-202, 249
organic fertilizers, 21, 249
outdoor shower, 35, 56, 69, 99, 101, 103, 123, 189, 192, 204
passive solar, 35, 249
path, 5, 38-39, 101, 159-160, 178, 249
paver blocks, 39, 159
peaceful personality, 151
peel, 89, 91-92, 249
perennial foods, 210
perfectionist personality, 127, 129, 147-148
permaculture, 5, 250, 255
pesticides, 11, 15, 25, 43, 49, 125, 127, 187-188, 197, 201-203, 213-214, 220, 227, 232, 237, 249
pizza, 87-88, 91-92
planning, 41, 43, 47, 175, 197, 207, 232, 243
plant safety, 242
play, 11, 13, 29, 57, 101, 213, 227, 231, 235
pollutants, 187, 189, 209
pollution, 192, 207, 227, 250
pond skimmer, 202
pond, 50, 53, 60, 63, 134, 183, 193-194, 196-198, 200-204, 209, 227
pressure regulator, 129-130, 136
pressure-compensating emitters, 129, 131, 136
properties, 171, 183, 190, 239, 250, 255
property owner questionnaire, 41-43, 45-47
property, 11, 13, 15, 19, 21, 23, 25, 27, 33, 41-43, 45-47, 53, 56-57, 59-60, 85, 95-97, 152, 156, 171, 183, 185, 187, 189-193, 197-198, 201-202, 204-205, 208-209, 211, 213-214, 225, 227, 235-237, 241-243, 245, 250, 255
pumps, 63, 69-70, 73, 95, 103, 134, 183, 187-189, 192, 201-202, 204, 249
rain barrel, 17, 183, 189, 250
rain garden, 17, 250
recycle, 2, 56, 123, 212, 225, 233
retaining walls, 18, 250
root rots, 135
rototilling, 20
rot-resistant hardwoods, 222, 250
rustic furniture, 107, 120, 123
safety, 51, 70, 138-139, 208, 235, 239-240, 242, 245, 251
self-mulch, 149, 170-171
sensitive environments, 237
shears, 49-50, 79, 129-131, 133, 136-137, 175
shrubs, 35, 50-51, 57, 96-97, 124, 148-149, 155, 157, 170, 179, 181, 199, 222, 231, 242, 248-249
sickle mowers, 53, 250
slope, 18, 190-191, 194-195, 243

slug damage, 129
soil scientist, 197
soil, 5, 18-20, 23, 41, 50, 59, 67, 81, 83, 101, 127, 129, 134-135, 138, 152, 156-157, 159, 163, 169, 179, 183, 191, 193, 195, 197, 201, 205, 209, 211, 219, 224, 232, 235, 237, 243, 249-250, 255
solar electric fence, 65-67, 95
solar panels, 60, 65, 67, 69-70, 73, 75, 95, 250
solarize, 156, 250
spring-fed, 197
stepping stones, 159
stone mulch, 127
string trimmers, 51, 172, 250
surface water, 192
surveys, 42, 245
sustainability, 5, 15, 17, 47, 59, 220
sustainable landscape investment, 11
swales, 60, 183, 191, 193-195, 204, 209, 250
synthetic weed barrier, 250
synthetic, 127, 156-157, 159, 197, 201, 250-251
system, 2, 19, 30, 42-43, 73, 77, 79, 129, 133-135, 138-139, 144, 183, 187, 189, 248
systems, 2, 17, 19, 25, 30, 42-43, 50, 60, 73, 77, 129, 133-136, 138-139, 144, 157, 183, 185, 188, 189, 217, 242, 248, 250-251
tanks, 11, 103, 134, 139, 183, 190-191, 193, 204, 224, 248
temperature, 37, 53, 87-88, 130, 138, 156, 201, 207, 247
tenon, 113, 115, 118-119, 141, 250
tenon-cutting, 117-119, 141, 143
tenon-making tool, 113, 115, 251
tool holder, 140-141
tool storage, 141, 143-144, 147
tools, 30, 49-51, 53, 65, 69, 73, 79-80, 103, 107, 113, 115, 117-119 129-131, 133, 136, 138, 140-145, 147, 159, 163, 167, 175, 179, 232, 239-240, 248, 251
torches, 51
toxic, 127, 171, 192, 235, 242
transitional areas, 37
true benefit, 15,17, 183, 248, 250
walkway, 38, 226
water storage, 183, 187, 204, 209
water supply, 79, 133-134, 139, 209
water tanks, 204
weed smothering, 167, 179
weed whackers, 172, 250
weed whips, 51, 172, 250
weeds, 20, 26, 29, 51, 65, 67, 127-128, 151-153, 155-157, 159, 166-167, 169, 172-173, 178-179, 210-211, 224, 232, 250
wetlands, 183, 185
wood carrier, 27

About the Author

Tom Girolamo is an expert on developing environmentally friendly, sustainable landscapes for residential and commercial properties in the United States. His unique approach for combining the property owners' personality with the applied sciences of agriculture, soil, water, and forestry to create sustainable landscapes that fit the owner's lifestyle sets Tom apart from all the others in professional landscaping.

He has developed a range of products, services, and methods (some which are patented and trademarked) that are in use all over the United States and are making inroads internationally. Tom's systems-based approach to sustainable landscapes allows one person to accomplish more work than standard landscape crews of six people … in the same amount of time. Small, specialized equipment, light-weight materials, and environmentally sensitive methods allow the business end of creating the landscape to be sustainable too.

Tom grew up on the outskirts of the industrial city of Beloit, Wis. His appreciation for nature and growing things came from family camping trips and a one-acre truck garden on the family's property. "We were vegetarians before anyone knew what that meant, including us. If we didn't grow it or build it we probably didn't have it."

Tom put himself through school working for a home builder and received his Forestry Degree with emphasis in Forest Management and in Urban Forestry from the University of Wisconsin-Stevens Point in 1982. Part of his forestry degree study included time in the Black Forest region of Germany. He graduated from the Permaculture Design Course of The Permaculture Research Institute and is a certified permaculture instructor.

After working for the Wisconsin Department of Natural Resources and the U.S. Forestry Service, Tom was a municipal arborist with the City of Stevens Point, Wis. for five years prior to starting his own company in 1988. Tom founded his company, Eco-Building & Forestry, LLC, which provides design, consulting, and installation of sustainable landscapes locally, nationally, and internationally. He is also the founder of Landscape For Life Foundation, Inc., a non-profit organization providing leading-edge leadership in education and training methods for generating repeatable, predictable results in sustainable landscapes for consumers in residential, commercial, and government lifestyle applications.

Tom and his wife, Kathy, live on seven and one-half acres of former alfalfa fields and cut-over woods that they have transformed into a healthy and diverse mix of uses. The property is called the Sustainable Landscape Center and you are welcome to make an appointment to visit.

MORE STEPS TO LIVING SIMPLY

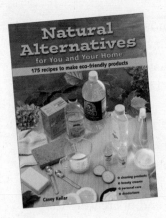

NATURAL ALTERNATIVES FOR YOU AND YOUR HOME

By Casey Kellar

From soaps and shampoos to fragrances and household cleaners this book outlines more than 175 recipes for making eco-friendly and cost-conscious products on your own. Using affordable ingredients that are easy to find, the detailed instructions and illustrations in this book guide you through successful creation of solutions that are good for you and for your home.

Softcover • 8¼ x 10⅞ • 208 p
Item#Z4649 • $24.99

THE EVERYTHING GUIDE TO HERBAL REMEDIES

By Martha Connors with Larry Altshuler, MD

This practical guide reveals the timeless healing power of the best herbs and natural remedies available today. Learn how to strengthen your immune system, ease hormonal mood swings, and treat such common ailments such as allergies and digestion problems.

Softcover • 8 x 9¼ • 304 p
Item# Z2760 • $15.95

365 WAYS TO LIVE GREEN

Your Everyday Guide to Saving the Environment

By Diane Gow McDilda

This easy-to-follow book will have you looking for ways to save the world before you get through the first section. Among the ideas explained are tips for finding hidden ingredients in bad-for-you-foods, ways to invest in "green" technology and what to look for when buying eco-friendly clothes and accessories.

Softcover • 5½ x 6¼ • 224 p
Item# Z2321 • $7.95

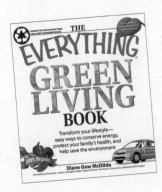

THE EVERYTHING GREEN LIVING BOOK

Transform Your Lifestyle

By Diane Gow McDilda; Foreword By Christopher J. Maro

This all-encompassing primer to practical tips, techniques and practices for embracing a "green" lifestyle is chock-full of ideas for transforming the way you live, work, travel and enjoy the environment. From simple steps like using nontoxic cleaning supplies and eating more organic foods, to volunteering during Earth Day events and eco-improvement efforts in your community, are discussed in this insightful and inspiring book.

Softcover • 8 x 9¼ • 320 p
Item#Z1288 • $14.95

Order directly from the publisher at **www.krausebooks.com**

Krause Publications, Offer **ACB9**
P.O. Box 5009
Iola, WI 54945-5009
www.krausebooks.com

Call **800-258-0929** 8 a.m. - 5 p.m. to order direct from the publisher, or visit booksellers nationwide or home improvement stores and garden centers.

Please reference offer **ACB9** with all direct-to-publisher orders